Time and History

Biblical Encounters Series

Suffering by Erhard S. Gerstenberger and Wolfgang Schrage
Translated by John E. Steely

Festival and Joy by Eckhart Otto and Tim Schramm
Translated by James L. Blevins

World and Environment by Odil Hannes Steck

Death and Life by Otto Kaiser and Eduard Lohse
Translated by John E. Steely

Faith by Hans-Jürgen Hermisson and Eduard Lohse
Translated by Douglas Stott

Achievement by Antonius H. J. Gunneweg and
Walter Schmithals
Translated by David Smith

Time and History by Siegfried Herrmann
Translated by James L. Blevins

Time and History

Siegfried Herrmann

Biblical Encounters Series

Translated by James L. Blevins

ABINGDON
Nashville

ZEIT UND GESCHICHTE

© 1977 Verlag W. Kohlhammer GmbH

TIME AND HISTORY

Translation copyright © 1981 by Abingdon

Library of Congress Cataloging in Publication Data

HERRMANN, SIEGFRIED, 1926–
 Time and history.
 (Biblical encounters series)
 Translation of Zeit und Geschichte.
 Bibliography: p.
 1. History (Theology)—Biblical teaching. I. Title. II. Series.
 BS680.H47H4713   220.8'9'01   80-25323

ISBN 0-687-42100-4

MANUFACTURED BY THE PARTHENON PRESS AT
NASHVILLE, TENNESSEE, UNITED STATES OF AMERICA

To Marie-Louise Henry

in memory of our joint destiny in time and history,
this book is gratefully dedicated

Contents

PREFACE:
THE HISTORICAL
CIGAR

Preface: The Historical Cigar

Just as the first rays of sunlight broke through the cloud-bedecked
skies, the entire first Prussian army set forth with banners
unfurled and with the sound of drums beating, in one last assault
against the heights. This powerful thrust of the Prussian reserve
cavalry had King Wilhelm bei Lipa, himself, at its head. Arranged
in broad half circles, the Prussian force easily pushed back the
courageous cavalry of the opposing Austrians and won the victory.
One eyewitness reported that the Austrians broke rank and fled
toward the river Elbe, as wild animals fleeing before a raging
forest fire. The Saxons were almost the only ones to hold their
position. Thousands found watery graves in the river or in the
flooded lowlands stretching out before the walls of Königgrätz.
The Prussians greeted their old king on the field of victory with
thundering acclamation. Later that evening, near the city of
Problus, the king met the crown prince and in a very moving
ceremony placed his own "order of the cross" around the prince's
neck. This great Prussian victory came at the cost of nearly 9,000
men, but this was small in contrast to the Austrian army which
was almost completely decimated. The Austrians lost over 44,000
men, including almost 20,000 prisoners, 11 banners, and 174
cannons. The Saxons gave up 1500 men but only one cannon.

With these words, Otto Kaemmel, professor and associate
rector of the Dresden Königlichen Gymnasium, described the
turning point and final outcome of the battle for Königgrätz,
which took place in the summer of 1866 [6:1234].* His book
titled *History of Germany* was published in 1889 and contained
1266 pages. Past generations have presented "history"
essentially as paving the way for the political development of
states. The high points of such development always take place
in mighty events on the battlefield. Not only are the fates of
peoples decided there, but solutions are sought there also for
the "smaller" conflicts brought about by thirst for revenge, lust

*The numbers in brackets refer to the entries in the Bibliography.

for prestige and power, and desire to demonstrate superiority. All these feelings merge together in a mass movement leading to armed conflict, with the ultimate expectation of aquisition of the enemy's goods—the so-called booty of war—including the annexation of lands, people, and possessions of all kinds. Victory demands its tribute, and the enemy has to pay—an ancient law of life.

The colorful picture of battle that Professor Kaemmel places before the eyes of his readers makes use of all the images needed to depict that great moment. The sun breaks through dark clouds; drums are beating; the whole army sets out for the last attack, with the king leading the way. The enemy fights courageously but ultimately must flee. One eyewitness described the flight as "wild animals fleeing before the forest fire." And the dear professor from Dresden, whose fellow countrymen were present, but not on the side of the victors, did not fail to add, "The Saxons were almost the only ones to hold their position." In addition, we encounter a gloomy picture of thousands killed in battle or drowned. Things brighten again as we witness the jubilation for the victor. And then in the fading light of the waning day, the old king honors the crown prince, who as everyone knows, entered the battle late, according to the exact plans of General Moltke, but not too late for his army to decide the battle. The casualties were very high and noted exactly by the chronicler. The losses of the victors stand in stark contrast with those of the defeated—9,000 Prussians over against 44,000 Austrians. The Saxons lost "only" 1500 men and only one cannon (why should that lost cannon even have been mentioned?).

That barbaric event, fought among German-speaking people, took place more than a century ago in northern Bohemia near Königgrätz and Sadowa. It was European history in the making. France and Italy were in the background; two years previously, Prussia had attempted to resolve the problem of Schleswig-Holstein in the German-Danish war of 1864. The battle at Königgrätz was praised as a victory of weapon techniques. The introduction of firing-pin weapons into the Prussian army and the refusal of Kaiser Franz Joseph to make use of those weapons gave the Prussians the advantage. Above all, however, the names of Prussians became indelibly inscribed upon the European consciousness—especially that of Moltke, whose classic example of battle strategy offered a grand illustration of his motto "March apart but fight together." It was "a strategic masterpiece—a repetition of the Battle of Waterloo," as one serious textbook commentator termed it [1:97]. Many anecdotal details of the king's role in the battle also made a deep impression on the people. He had thrown himself into the fray—Bismarck had been forced to hold him back. Hermann Jahnke, author of many patriotic books, reported,

> Full of uneasiness, the king looked toward the heights northeast of Chlum where the attack of the crown prince's army was to take place. At some distance, Bismarck waited, seated on his mount, thinking similar thoughts. His overcoat was thrown back so that one could see the uniform of a Prussian militia cuirassier major. Then Bismarck saw Moltke, that master of the battlefield, seated in unequaled calmness on his steed. He rode over to him to inquire concerning his view of things. As silent as the mysterious Sphinx, Moltke gazed into the distance. Bismarck offered him his cigar case which contained only two cigars, one with a damaged wrapper and the other in good condition. The master of the art of war took the good one and left the other for the genius of the art of politics. When Bismarck returned to the king, he reported: "Everything must be going well; for Moltke had the nerve at this decisive moment to select the better cigar from my case!" [5:425, 6].

This tale about the cigar leaves its imprint on the mind and is very much a part of the story of Königgrätz. When Wolfgang Liebeneiner, a well-known motion picture director, filmed the story of Bismarck in the early 1940s, his purpose was to help the sorely tested German people keep alive the memory of Bismarck's great kingdom. In doing so, he did not leave out the story of Königgrätz and Bismarck's cigar case. Only color film could have shown the difference in the wrappings of the two cigars, and since only black and white technology was available at the time, the distinction was made with a big cigar and a little cigar. If that scene had been left out, the memory of the battle of Königgrätz would have been incomplete.

Such details eventually become a part of national tradition and provide a way for the people to celebrate their heroes, while recognizing their weaknesses; to honor their great men and at the same time to express their sympathy toward them. More recent historical writing makes little of such anecdotes—history viewed as a collection of "little tales." Rudolf Buchner's work, *German History in its European Framework* (1975), places great emphasis on the year 1866, but the events themselves shrink into short wire service-like reports:

> Because of the training of the Prussian army, and its superior modern firing weapons, and above all the strategic genius of Moltke, who led the three separate armies into one striking force, the battle was quickly won in a "blitzkrieg" type operation, on the fields outside Königgrätz. Within three weeks Austria fell. Bismarck overplayed the danger of the intervention of France and brought about a "blitz peace" to follow the "blitzkrieg." Austria was forced to withdraw from Germany and lost Venice to Italy, but otherwise was unharmed. Bismarck carried out these mild conditions with all eagerness in order to please the king, who thought Austria should be punished [2:340].

Of course, in 1866, no one had heard of a blitzkrieg, let alone a "blitz peace." However, the quick battles of that century were sometimes carried out in blitzkrieg fashion, whether in eighteen or fewer days. The word "blitzkrieg," at one time used in propaganda, is now an expression in serious historical writing—even where one would not expect to see it. However, the results of that "blitz peace" should not be overlooked. Prussia very decisively underlined its claim to leadership and power. Austria was removed in a conclusive way from the potential German kingdom. The victor's decree outlined a process which reached its climax and provisional conclusion in the "establishment of the Reich" following the hostilities against France in 1870–71. By 1866, at the latest, one can see the "German kingdom" beginning to form under the leadership of Prussia.

The battle of 1866, with which we began this discussion, and which at first glance might be seen as an amusing paradigm of national historical writing, on closer inspection becomes the cornerstone of Prussian-German historical consciousness. The Kaiser, Bismarck, and Moltke were the blacksmiths of the kingdom, welding together the vessel of "enthusiasm for the fatherland" with which one set out to the battlefield in 1914, and which seemed not to have been lost even at the war's conclusion in 1918. Under changed presuppositions, the idea of the fatherland continued to dominate and was expressed in new forms. It emerged in the conflicts of the political parties, with their various interests, and finally found expression in the very enticing symbolism of National Socialism. The idea of the fatherland was so persuasive because it presented itself as a logical consequence of historical continuity.

The Third Reich viewed itself as a new expression of the German idea of the Reich that had evolved as a unique historical construction under the Saxon Kaiser Heinrich I. By consolidating the German principalities, he brought about the first unified political entity. Heinrich's First Reich then was replaced by Bismarck's creation, known as the Second Reich, although that designation did not play an important role at the time, since it came into being only after reflection concerning the establishment of the Third Reich. The events that were part of the "idea of the Reich" and its prior history now became a part of that red thread running throughout German history and are still very much a part of our consciousness. The Third Reich perceived the necessity and the possibility of using the idea of the Reich as a concept of the "German nation" in the service of political persuasion. In addition to literature, the medium of film proved to be an excellent way to present German history. There were films of Frederick and Bismarck so impressive that they continued to be effective on through the war years and had a great following.

In these films, "history" was not presented as remembrance of the past—a collection of anecdotes strung together—but to a great degree, was seen as the self-presentation of the German people. Of course, this was an attempt to demonstrate that the everyday policies and goals of the government should be seen in continuity with the great traditions and could be legitimatized when viewed in relation to "history." One might reject this intent to propagandize, but one could not overlook the attempt to introduce a national identity—a feeling of sharing in the nation's history—which assured the widespread success and influence of the historical films.

The concept of "nation," which reaches its highest expression when linked to the adjective "indivisible," has been linked closely to the development of the European national states since the nineteenth century. In the "German Reich," it received the unified form of political entity when the famous edict which founded the Reich was issued in the Hall of Mirrors in the Versailles Palace, on January 18, 1871. This act so influenced the nationalistic feeling of the people that when Germany was divided after 1945, it was viewed as an unlawful deed perpetrated upon the nation. The slogan "reunification" has as its goal the restoration of the 1937 borders, or the basic lines of Bismarck's kingdom, with the exception of the annexations affected after 1938 in an attempt to establish a "Greater Germany."

These considerations bring us close to the most direct and fateful form of the concept of "history." In that form, one avoids

every kind of evaluation. It is certain that the division of
Germany was a fate whose gravity can be perceived only when
viewed in relation to the fact that the historical act of founding a
kingdom in 1871 was virtually annulled in 1945. This kingdom
will not be restored in the foreseeable future, no matter what
direction events take. However, the tensions of the present
should not be seen apart from the chain of unequaled
revolutionary changes which came about in the Prussian-German Reich between 1871 and 1945, shaking it and finally
destroying it. Thereby we have touched only the fringe of that
very serious fatalistic question for which untold sacrifices were
made. Such self-giving was required by two world wars and
their aftermaths, not to mention the meaningless murder and
ideological delusion brought about for racial and political
reasons, within and outside the German territories. Bloodbaths
have played disruptive roles in all periods of human history.
This is a fact that always indicates a need for expiation, but this
need diminishes in significance when murder and threat of
death become obvious legitimate means for the conduct of
political power. Following on the heels of technical progress is
the potential power for the destruction of people and property.
The firing-pin weapons of 1866 were trifles in comparison to the
modern weaponry of warfare. Less than a hundred years ago,
the king, riding his mount, could appear in the crowded streets
among his people. What modern potentate would risk that
today?

The scale of the present can be determined only when
delineated with the measuring rod of the past. What is attained
in a certain period therefore always is relative, because gains
and losses in the historical realm can be only relative. What one
generation creates, the next destroys. A generation will restore
and be proud of what it has accomplished, not realizing that
most of what it has done was already there. In fact, all the pains
taken in restoration could have been avoided simply by
preserving what was accomplished by previous generations.

The natural course of generation following generation gives rise to the pendulum swing of "history." One perceives it for the most part in sorrowful experiences, because of one's own very nature. Opening one's ears to the past remains an art, for in order to grasp the past, one must presume a readiness for identification with it and, not least of all, a knowledge of it. Remembering the values, experiences, and weaknesses of the past is difficult, in most cases, because to know and to bear the burden of the past is a very heavy responsibility. The average person indeed finds it a very unpleasant task. One is confronted with too many details and facts about some previous hazy time, and this causes one to become weary and stumble. For most people a certain haziness with regard to history begins when they try to reflect upon the decades preceding their own birth. Historical remembrance therefore is actually one's own business—a task that is inclined to be pedagogical. Politicians practice it, and idealists often falsify it. Each generation must learn anew that humanity learns about it itself through historical knowledge.

The difficulties we encounter in understanding ourselves in the second half of this century arise, not least of all, from a broken relationship with time and history. This is especially true of the German people, who have lost the ability to perceive their own history objectively. The downfall in 1945 caused a complete loss of identity. Not only did one's national past come to an end but the continuity of a whole value-system was shattered and placed in a twilight zone. The people so often referred to as the nation of "poets and scholars" found it difficult to recover that image and became entangled in contradictions and errors. Fear of a new "nationalism" suppressed a healthy concern for "the nation." It seemed unfitting to be overly concerned about "national" values. It was more comfortable to express oneself in terms that transcended the national; that were more in tune with foreign feelings and expressions. It seemed to be appropriate at the time to be fully open to the

Western world, especially America. It seemed only right to be
tied to one of the leading world powers.

Germany's past was treated quite differently in the section
occupied by the Eastern power. German history was
subordinated to all the measures of ideology of the officially
prescribed world-view. Was it not too great a burden to place
on the generation of the two world wars, to expect them to
adapt to a new democratic state structure, after already
experiencing monarchy, a republic, and finally, dictatorship?
Was it not too much to ask them to express their "values of
history" in yet new forms?

On January 18, 1971—on the one-hundredth anniversary
of the Kaiser's proclamation at Versailles, which had brought
forth the Reich under Bismarck's influence—that "Reich"
found itself wrecked, reduced in size, and divided. On one side
it was led by Marxists and on the other by Social Democrats. In
no circumstance would that have met with Bismarck's favor.
Nevertheless, the chancellor of West Germany in 1971 once
again raised the concept of "nation," and his government
worked on a political solution for all of Germany that would
alleviate the harshness of the wall of division and allow more
access across it. January 18, 1971, was no day of rejoicing but
rather a day of massive reflection, although it found no
perceptible echo among the general public. The German
Association of Publishers commemorated the event with an
illustrated volume dealing with those one hundred years of
German history and included a historical analysis of that
period. The foreword to the volume was written by Richard von
Weizsäcker, and the following postscript was added by Willy
Brandt, then chancellor of West Germany.

It is very painful and discomforting to look back over one hundred
years of German history. Nevertheless it need not be
discouraging. . . . The question concerning the future can
receive a positive answer if we Germans develop the capability to

reflect, apart from our emotions, upon the causes of our defeat and draw from these reflections reasonable political lessons [4:406].

These words were quite appropriate but their suggestion was most difficult to follow. To separate oneself from one's emotions may be possible as an academic exercise but in actuality one never quite reaches that ideal. It is even harder to realize political consequences apart from emotion. The words of the former chancellor are easy to understand; yet they illustrate the extent of the conflict that always exists between historical knowledge and political reality. It is indeed a conflict that cannot be avoided.

Gustav Heinemann, president of the German Republic at that time, and also a Social Democrat, addressed the nation on television on the eve of January 18. As a leader in both church and political affairs, he also set forth the thought that "one must reflect on the causes of defeat apart from emotion," but that at the same time, one must draw "historical conclusions" from them. He placed the event of 1871 within two political coordinates as he sought to clarify the prior history and evaluation of the event. In so doing he also pointed to other possibilities and difficulties of analyzing the German nation. Heinemann said,

We have been called a late developing nation. In fact, we did achieve national unity (1871) much later and less completely than other nations. The cry for unity arose in the wars of liberation against Napoleon, principally among the restless students at the Wartburg festival of 1817, among the people gathered to celebrate at the Hambach castle in 1832, and finally by the storm and pressure of the people in 1848/49. However, each time a voice arose from one of the dozens of princely states, it was suppressed and Germany remained shattered. Should we celebrate 1871? Emanuel Geibel has expressed the feelings of many others in his poem which is found in many German school books:

"Just as Pallas Athena sprang from Jupiter's head,
so sprang the Reich, ready for war, from Bismarck's
head."

Bismarck is represented as one who created unity by means of
blood and iron—at least this is the way it is taught and
represented in countless statues of him dotting the German
countryside. We must recognize that such a view is an
over-simplification and that as such it should be treated with
suspicion. Every such simplification contains both truth and
error. In 1871, Bismarck forced the union of small princely states,
with the exception of those Germans who lived in Austria.
However, Bismarck did not belong in the ranks of those who were
waving the "red-gold-black" colors of a united Germany, desiring
both unification and democracy. One who draws a line connecting
the wars of liberation and Wartburg with Hambach, St. Paul's
church at Frankfurt, on to Rastatt, as the last station of the
revolution of 1848/49, and then continues the line on to Sedan and
Versailles, completely distorts history. In our national anthem,
written by Hoffmann von Fallersleben (1841), a believer in
democracy, we sing of unity, justice, and freedom. In its first
days, the Weimar Republic also sang that anthem! In the kingdom
of the Kaiser, up until 1918, the people sang "Hail to the One
Wearing the Crown of Victory."

When the German Reich was called into being at Versailles
one hundred years ago, not one of the 1848 group was present.
Indeed, men such as August Bebel, and Wilhelm Liebknecht,
and other social democrats who had expressed their feelings
against the nationalistic excesses of the victory over France, all sat
in prison. Around the Kaiser in Versailles stood the princes, the
generals, the high officials, but no representatives of the people.
The birth of the Reich destroyed the links between nationalism
and democracy. The German national consciousness was tied
securely to the monarchial conservative powers, which in the
previous decades had stood stubbornly in the way of the
democratic forces.

No one will dispute that in setting forth this line of argument,
Heinemann consciously tried to reinterpret a view of German
history that is becoming current or that already is current. For a

line running from the wars of liberation of 1871 to the year 1918, and on from there to the end of the unified national state in 1945 (although this latter period actually should not be included), very extensively dominates our German view of history. In any case this is the way it is presented almost exclusively in the textbooks of our schools. The other line, which we will call the democratic one, reflects more accurately the desire of the men of 1848 and stands in contrast to the reality of 1871. This special concept must be addressed and viewed as a thoroughly unconventional train of thought. It was this thought that the chancellor of Germany sought to bring before the German people for their reflection.

This is not the place to enter into a critique of this short sketch, or to question the correctness and historical reliability of the proposed shift of emphasis in the formative forces of Germany as set forth there. Whether the establishment of the Reich in 1871 really destroyed the link between the democratic and the national intent, or whether the German national consciousness was firmly bound to monarchial conservative forces, are highly explosive conclusions that are still being questioned. We have made no mention as to which presuppositions calculated to bring about a real democratic condition were important to the German people themselves between 1871 and 1918. The statements of the Dresden Gymnasium professor quoted in the introduction indicate that he counted himself among the losers of 1866, but they do not conceal that he shared in the Prussian victory. The positive stance of Germany toward monarchial forms of government was certainly always a part of its past, and during the period of the monarchs this tendency was not seen as a negative characteristic. The constitutional monarchy allowed room for the democratic forces but did not allow them much influence in the business of government. However, it did create an affection for their princes in the people and the end of the monarchy in 1918 did not result in entirely positive evaluations among thoughtful critics. In other European lands the monarchy continued and played an important role.

One ought not to debate the right of a politician to establish one view of the past based on his own experience and his own independent insights. However, the difficulty presented in such speeches of reflection is unavoidable. History is shown as the justification of that which has been attained. The facts of the past appear ordered around a goal—a particular point in the present which is to be highlighted, interpreted, or understood. The contrast to other points of view is brought out and made into a problem in order to present the envisioned picture of history convincingly. This type of thing occurred in Heinemann's discriminating evaluation of the parallel development of active forces. In any case, it served him as evidence of a historical continuum, be it in his criticism of the traditional view of the movement of monarchical-conservative powers or in his bemoaning of the break with the democratic line of development represented by the men of 1848–49.

The question concerning the continuity and legitimacy of historical developments allows the concern for history to be an important and unavoidable task which reaches into the intellectual debates of every age. The determination of one's own place is impossible without a knowledge of the past; but it also involves an evaluation of the past. This evaluation cannot exclude the view of present forms of the state, society, or the respective intellectual environment. The course of succeeding generations serves to remind us of the need to become a part of the continuum of historical movement. Whoever breaks with his past, or has his past broken for him, sees himself immediately on uncertain ground and is moved to find and confirm his identity in some new, or other, continuum. An intended break with the past sooner or later proves to be a self-delusion. Even when it appears that a break has succeeded, as a rule, one must pay for it dearly. In the dimensions of world history, such success is usually bound up with considerable spilling of blood as a result of wars or revolutions.

As far as German history is concerned, the events that took place before and after 1871 should not be seen by us today as a break with history or as a fateful breaking of a historical continuum. The actual points of crisis that seem to support a judgment concerning discontinuity can be found in the years 1918, 1933, and 1945—each in a different degree. That problem also concerned the publishers of the special edition quoted above—Hans-Adolf Jacobsen and Hans Dollinger. They wrote in their foreword to the volume:

> Among the numerous problems of German politics, the discussion of continuity and discontinuity deserves special consideration. . . . In the Weimar Republic, a primary concern of foreign policy was to establish once again a sovereign big power status. The inner weaknesses of this Republic would finally lead to the collapse of the first German experiment in democracy. Its primary goal pointed more to the past than to the future. This goal was always expressed in the traditional categories of power politics found in other countries. Viewed in this way, the element of continuity dominated even though the means and methods of accomplishing it were always conditioned by the times. Above all, as a result of the numerous world revolutions of our century brought about by a radical spirit in the masses and the unceasing march of science and technology, a qualitative change took place in the present setting of goals. That fact should lead us to speak of discontinuity since 1933, rather than continuity [4:10].

It is obvious that the example of our own land's problems should be introduced here and placed in the bright light of historical judgment. It should be clear to what extent history and historical activity represent an existential task quite distant from work that is centered around an academician's desk. History is a part of ourselves. We are bound up in historical movements that, not least of all, mold our own lives. If this fact is basically conceded, then we can understand that opinions vary concerning the evaluation of history—or even more precisely, that the movements of the past, which we ourselves did not help to shape, are nevertheless very important for the understanding of the present and the assessment of the future. The well informed will readily perceive that in this short outline of German history, which has been used here for the purpose of example, we have encountered known, as well as unknown questions and problems that concern present-day historical research and lead to the so-called crisis of historical research. In the following sections, it is not our purpose to deal in a thorough manner with the actual or theoretical questions of the science of history. However, it should be clear that in encountering the biblical facts, the problems of history and the writing of history are much more graphic than one might meet elsewhere in a purely abstract-theoretical treatment. Thus the encounter with historical problems—especially those arising from the biblical text and from biblical research—can be understood as a possible contribution to the theoretical deliberations of historical research.

A.
THE ENCOUNTER: HISTORICAL RESEARCH AND BIBLICAL TRADITION

Introduction

In order to give an overview of the questions and methods of historical consideration and research, and at the same time to give a profile of the encounter with biblical facts, we shall outline five steps of our method of being concerned and involved with what we call "history." Five essential fields of labor, which can be developed according to necessity, or according to one's liking, stand before the historian, or one who is inclined to historical thinking: (1) historical research; (2) the portrayal of history; (3) the hermeneutic of history; (4) the philosophy of history; (5) the question concerning a, or the, transcendental purpose of history, which theologians refer to as "the theology of history." It should be added that the last two fields—the philosophy of history and the theology of history—might not be perceived in the same way by every historian. As a rule they are the concern of philosophers or theologians. That fact should not deny, however, that every attempt to understand history, either through the stages of its research or through its first portrayal of the facts, can lead one into the realms of philosophical or theological questioning. In confronting biblical history it is necessary to speak to this wide field of reference. It will be shown that this does not result from a subjective religious interest alone but from a certain inevitability arising from the subject itself presented by history. More clearly said, the events taking place in the realm of time and place in which men share, but for which they are not held solely responsible, provoke the question concerning the meaning and significance of historical movements. That brings about philosophical and theological questioning.

It should be expressly pointed out that consequently, the five fields just named should be kept separated, due to their systematic conceptions and for the sake of their methodological clarity. Actually, there is much similarity among them—they overlap one another and finally constitute an indissoluble relationship. For history does not exist in abstractions and is not an impersonal or superpersonal power. What we call history rests upon organic connections that come to us in the rivers of time—often, to be sure, in complex entanglements very difficult to unravel. The structure of our mental capabilities and our methods of thought cause us to perceive these entanglements at first only in part. We realize that we can approach the individual event from many different points. However, its complete scope of significance can be extracted only with difficulty. One's relationship to history therefore is bound up with partial experiences, which in turn produce partial knowledge. The more one succeeds in stripping away the layers of an event, the more one can determine precisely what causative factors were at work in producing the new effects. In any case, our judgment thus will be more certain.

In this connection it is instructive to discover that "history" was originally a plural form of the singular term, *Geschichte* or *Geschicht*. In Jablonski's *Allgemeine Lexikon der Künste und Wissenschaften* of 1748, the following definition is found: "History is a mirror of virtue and vice in which one can learn through a strange experience what to do or what to ignore" [11:22,3]. The pronounced pedagogical aspect disclosed in this definition still must be considered. At the moment, one may conclude that history in the sense of "that which happened," takes on the meaning of events and occurrences—narratives that in their limited scope reflect the world of experience of other people. Thus they furnish instructive examples for life. Only the sum of such "narratives" when placed in a larger context can clarify the interrelatedness of the events. The term "history," which has become an abstraction, is usually applied in colloquial speech to these interrelated events. The truth of history therefore cannot be cut off from the reality of its narratives or from the actuality of events. The discovery of this last truth is a unique matter, and therefore, one might say, one of the prime tasks of historical research. Let us now turn to a consideration of the first of the fields of endeavor listed earlier.

I. Historical Research

a. Tasks, Concepts, and Methods

Appropriately, "Historical Research" has been placed before "Portrayal of History." Of course, research as such is also portrayable, and its results can be adapted to measured description and can appear in the form of generally available and usable reports, essays, statistics, overviews, and commentaries. The presentation of the results of research, however, is not in any way the portrayal of history in its intended sense. The summarization of the results makes possible the portrayal of historical events and circumstances as they have emerged from individual research and later have been combined into a total picture.

What are the tasks of historical research? In first place, without a doubt, stands the study of records and documents, as well as extant written original testimonies of some period in time. These are not only the "notarized" attested acts of interested parties, the texts of agreements, arrangements, establishments, deeds, declarations, and so on. These documents are of unusual worth for the understanding of events, but they are limited in their use. They portray the complexity of a formularized condensed picture of past disputes whose presuppositions can only be explained by the actual course of events. The true task of historical research is to cast light on the events definitely attested to in the documents.

When we speak here of individual records, we refer to contemporary notices, newspaper reports, narratives, and summarizing presentations which also are to be viewed as highly valuable sources and even bear the signatures of their producers. One should distinguish between the report of an accidental witness, that of a commissioned reporter, and the later additions of a third-hand report of a redactor, correspondent, historian, writer, or politician. The number and type of those participating in the process of reporting is shown in the validity and point of view of what is being reported. If the event appears in various levels of observation, then the layers of the connections which once constituted "history" should be recognizable and accessible. The sum of that which is historical enters into history *(Geschichte)*.

The word "historical," which in colloquial usage no longer can be distinguished from the term *Geschichte*, still must be judged differently because of its point of origin. *Geschichte* is an old high-German word that can be traced back to the root *gisciht*, meaning an individual event or occurrence. *Historia* has its origin in Greek and comes to us through the Latin, signifying "that which is known about an event," or a report based on one's own, or someone else's, experience. In Homer, the *histor* is "one who knows"—a spy, an expert, a witness—hence the "knowledge of eyewitnesses," or knowledge brought about by viewing. Finally, the German word *wissen* goes back to this Indogermanic root, which is also expressed in the Greek *histor*, originally *wistor* (spelled with Digamma). Thus we can conclude that *historie* involves historical knowledge—information that comes to us about events. That which is "historical" is thus not every event, or every "narrative," but rather that which becomes knowledge or the material of knowledge—that which enters into "transmission and is declared to us through tradition" *(traditio)*.

Historical research, strictly speaking, is concerned with the investigation and evaluation of historical knowledge of that which has happened. There exists between the two concepts *Historie* and *Geschichte* that tension of what really happened, and the way it should be reported, and the way it should be portrayed in its historical sense, and how it became an object of transmission and tradition. For historical knowledge is only that which is transmitted through witnesses. Yet one must realize that even there, history has not been captured in terms of pure facts. From its very beginning, historical research involves the philosophical tension between the correctness of what was perceived and the correctness of its repetition in the mouth or through the pen of the reporting witness. In his report, and through the results of the seen or shared-in course of actions, either intended or unintended, the witness gives an understanding of causative connections which correspond to his own personal insights. It is to be hoped that they are accurate. A second reporting witness, if present, can correct the first or disclose any errors. It need not be added that a wide field separates a weakness in comprehension from a conscious distortion on the part of the reporting witness. This can present historical research with a multitude of riddles. Normally speaking, the subjective honesty of the witness is taken for granted. However, a complete report of historical events can be transmitted to us without our being able to ascertain the specific eyewitness. For the report of the witness still must be mediated through the "historian"—one who has gathered the transmitted knowledge and has brought it into a systematic order, factually and chronologically. For the event is inseparable from its place in time—from its "before" and "after." The simplest event demands its appropriate presentation, a didactical accomplishment related to the hearer or reader. For that reason it is not astonishing, but also not taken for granted that, in a very high measure, the most recent historical research has made the ways and means of reporting an independent object of its endeavors. It has learned to distinguish between the reporter and that which is reported; between the probability of events and the possible intention of their portrayal.

In more recent historical science, the catchword "historic" is used in a qualified sense. Without going into the wide implications of this concept, let it suffice to say that those concerns that are described as historic are, first of all, almost exclusively of a theoretical nature and are a "sub-discipline of historical science" [11:69]. There is a concern to develop a canon of methodical rules by which historical research is controllable in itself, and historical knowledge is at the same time transformable "within the framework of social practice" [11:83]. "Historic" is defined as "the systematic self reflection of historical science" (Rüsen) [11:63]. Very simply said, it is a matter of acquiring theoretical presuppositions of historical knowledge based on the extant sources. From these sources, the unique value of that which has been transmitted can be determined. In certain respects, that amounts to a certain process of subtraction. To subtract is to remove from a source that which can be traced back probably, or certainly, to secondary influences. Such tendencies begin in the subjective presuppositions and peculiarities of the author and continue into the formulation of those ideal, ideological, or philosophical concepts that are foreign infiltrations into that which is reported. Such attempts may be influenced by the skeptical belief that transmitted or portrayed history does not do justice, or falls short of perfection, in reference to the reported events. On the other hand, the real chance exists that the event we wish to recognize can be set free from transmitted concepts of value and can be presented in its own right, free of any value system. And if the occasion should arise, the event also might find new value through other categories of evaluation.

One finds it extremely difficult to deny the strict logic of such deliberations. However, at the same time, one must question the possibilities, limitations, and goals of this highly rationalistic dissecting of the transmitted texts. One also can question whether in this way one actually has recovered history in its respective actual worth. What is left, after the subtraction process takes place? After additions by the author and by other prevailing circumstances are removed from the historical source of testimony, what is left, as the desirable and available goal of impartial factual research?

Let us now turn from abstract expressions to the more concrete. German history during the last one hundred years, which was brought into our discussions in a fitting and paradigmatic way in the introduction, offers considerable difficulty in historical research. The overwhelming number of various sources makes it difficult for any one historian to master them all. "Master" here, however, does not mean reading alone or selecting, evaluating, or presenting; it means understanding this source material against its respective presuppositions—the intrinsic value of its own historical developments that conditioned and influenced one another in that turbulent period of time. It is obvious that the course of events in Prussia, Germany, and Europe was not broad enough to incorporate all forces at work in the situation. The components that were mentioned in the speech of Gustav Heinemann, and which incorporated a series of emphatic events that occurred between 1813 and 1945, can provide only the simplest framework for the unusually complex power relationships. To those political and military developments, one undoubtedly must add the increasing political party development within the states of Europe. These parties in turn were the result of social relationships in a time of unfolding modern industry and the development of large firms. Technical progress was enjoyed but was experienced at the price of enduring the full awakening of the materialistic control of one's being—not just in warfare, with its immediate extensive destruction, but also in the development of agriculture, the growth of large cities, the increase of factory work, the division of work, the move from country to city, and the loss of tradition and custom. The intellectual results are well known. A materialistic technical expansion brought about a shrinking of general intellectual life and a rapid reduction of humanistic and, above all, religious value-systems. It became more and more difficult to obtain an overview of the greater political and economic connections. The masses were ripe for ideological indoctrination. The emptying of the fixed value-system of the intellectual world allowed seductive forces to increase the measure and inclination of their ideological delusion. Hitler's Germany unfolded on the broadest of stages and should be understood as the result of the most extensive aberrations.

The sources available to the researcher are legion, but the categories available for mastering the material are not equally at the command of every researcher. Next to the historian of political history stands the specialist in economic and social history. Cultural and intellectual history is complicated enough, but we cannot overlook the specialized work of the historians of music, literature, and art. In that period, church history and the stance of Christian faith appear to be almost on a side track, as an *l'art pour l'art* undertaking, which could, to a certain degree, be dispensed with. This is true despite the work of Ritschl, Harnack, Rudolf Otto, Karl Barth, Otto Dibelius, Martin Niemoeller, and Rudolf Bultmann, which aroused public interest beyond the church and other special branches of study.

This short overview of the most recent past has been in specific reference to Germany, but with new conceptions and postulates it well could be applied to all of Europe and to the rest of the world, making clear the dilemma with which the historian is confronted. The impossibility of finding everything in the original sources leads one to secondary sources, or to so-called interdisciplinary research—to methods and perceptions that at times are practical elsewhere, in reference to specific material and research principles. Research into these sources must by necessity limit itself to small comprehensible units, seek attainable goals, and be in harmony with the documents of tradition.

Therein is found the dilemma of the most recent historical research, in the sense of a classical discipline of history, and it has become almost impossible to abandon the professional historian to that triad of political history, economic history, and cultural history. Specialization has gone so far that these divisions presume their own special knowledge and abilities and cannot be mastered or researched by any one scholar. In addition, each of these individual researchers must be aware of historical contexts without which his results might appear to be isolated or wrongly interpreted. The historian must from time to time develop technically related concepts and categories, in accordance with the subject, but also must be open to communicate with other historical relationships and disciplines, if he wishes to be theoretically correct in all tasks. Thus a history of music of the nineteenth century might be representative of the music culture of its time, even though one might not see obvious political movements within it. Interpretation remains a wide field.

b. Ancient Sources and Biblical Texts

What we have said about the difficulties that confront modern historical research in the most recent past, and the problems involved in mastering these difficulties, also can be applied to the more distant past. Appearances deceive, if one believes that scientific inquiry must have been much easier in the past because the sources were not as complex. There are sufficient sources, but they are not extensive enough to give valid answers to all the questions that must be asked. No one doubts that life in ancient times was less complex and complicated than ours; yet no less effort is required for understanding that period than is demanded in later periods. As is well known, the researcher of ancient times could not rely upon well-ordered archives to help open up the sources. Ancient literature was scattered widely about, philologically speaking, not extensively developed, and saturated in idioms; all of which presumes an independent study in that discipline if one desires to understand it. These sources often have sections missing and are fragmentary in nature. Tablets and papyri are often incomplete or are discovered only accidentally. In addition to research done behind a desk, one also should mention the more recent excavations and explorations of ancient sites and buildings, for what is discovered is of utmost interest. When one can find no written sources, then the silent sources of archeology become significant in reference to the knowledge they afford. In order to understand, to analyze, and to preserve these, historical research must come into contact with architectural research, art history, and the possibilities afforded by chemical and photographic techniques and methods of research. However, this is not the place to fill in those kinds of details. But within the framework of the subject of this book, this is the place to encounter the Bible. The testimonies of the Old and New Testaments are transmitted to us as objects of research—a part of ancient literature—and as such they are embedded in the cultural and intellectual world of the Near East. This testimony covers about 1300 years, or perhaps somewhat more, if one reckons the time from the onset of the oral tradition.

The source value of the biblical tradition is of great importance. The proof leading to this perception cannot be captured in a few words, but is the end result of interdisciplinary endeavors. This work began unintentionally in a period of time when this modern concept had not been clearly demarcated. To be sure, the historical worth of the biblical sources has never been placed in question, apart from challenges by outsiders, who quite often were influenced by ideological or anti-religious premises, or were motivated by a desire to devalue the Bible. They did not ponder the fact, or perhaps did not know, that the biblical writings are for the most part older than the oldest records of Greek and Roman history. The transmitted manuscripts of individual biblical books are among the most reliable sources we possess from the ancient world. In more recent times, the discovery of biblical manuscripts at the ancient site of Qumran, by the Dead Sea, confirms that fact in regard to the Old Testament (the oldest documents go back to the second century B.C.). In the New Testament area, we have long possessed manuscripts dating back to the second century A.D., which contain texts from the Gospels.

The facts of the biblical writings also have been confirmed by the interdisciplinary endeavors mentioned above. This type of work has been done especially in Near Eastern studies. In the first stages of this work, the Egyptian hieroglyphics were decoded by the Frenchman Champollion (1822); then the Persian writings were translated, and later the Babylonian-Assyrian cuneiform script, under the direction of the German, Grotefend (since 1802). In the course of untold minute work, it became more and more possible to read the old texts with precision and to enrich and secure old knowledge by the introduction of new discoveries. One might remember, in this regard, the deciphering (in the year 1930) of the so-called Ugaritic, a writing using cuneiform script based on the foundation of an "alphabet" used in the northern Syrian city-state of Ugarit, around the middle of the second millennium B.C. The possibility of reading this source allowed the researcher a direct view into the problems of the world of the Old Testament—namely, into the religious and administrative problems. No less important was the new knowledge gained about the Hittites. The script and language of that people of Asia Minor also date from the second millenium B.C.;

Hittite power and influence reached as far as Syria. As one of the big powers, it concluded a treaty of peace with King Ramses II of Egypt.

The opening up of the ancient oriental sources, which included written records on various kinds of writing materials, as well as archaeological testimonies of all kinds, along with the comprehensive portrayal of Greek and Latin historical writing, brought about a complete picture of the course of history in the lands between the Persian gulf and the Mediterranean, and also between the highlands of Asia Minor and Iran, to the Sudan. This picture was made complete by combining the knowledge from the Hittite sources with that gained from the Greek and Roman. Archeological layers such as those at Jericho, dating back as far as the older Stone Age (about 7000 B.C.), could be confirmed and afforded considerable insight regarding the historical development of succeeding periods. The emergence of readable linguistic records was not due primarily to the perfection of written language but was the result of critical evaluation of historical events. Egypt arrived at that state of record-keeping in the third millennium B.C., but Mesopotamia did not reach that point until a somewhat later time. We cannot speak here of the detailed course of that history, but the affirmation must be made that the Old Testament fits into this picture of ancient oriental history in a very convincing way, without any significant seam. This is true especially after the sojourn of the Israelite tribes in Egypt under Ramses II (1290–1224 B.C.). The previous period in the Old Testament—that of the Patriarchs, Abraham, Isaac, and Jacob—belongs to the second millenium B.C., but it is still debatable whether this was in the beginning, the middle, or the second half of that period. Without a doubt the historicity of these forms is certain. The last witnesses of the Old Testament belong unmistakably to the first half of the second century B.C. The apocalyptic pictures of chapter 7 of Daniel point to the writer as one who was a contemporary of the Syrian ruler,

Antiochus IV, Epiphanes. Antiochus IV was influenced by the spirit of later Greece and interfered in and had no regard for the cultural life surrounding the Jerusalem temple. His goal was to introduce the hellenistic spirit among the Jews. The decisive resistance of the Maccabees—those Jews who truly followed the Law—led to the establishment of the Hasmonean dynasty. The Hasmonean period also was punctuated by a chain of heroic bloody events and reached its final defeat in the period after the canonization of the Old Testament. The appearance of the Romans in Palestine is reflected in the testimonies of the so-called Apocryphal writings, but also constitutes the background for the entire New Testament—the Gospels, the Epistles, and the Revelation of John.

The real problem of biblical historiography and its study is no longer one involving the inner relationships of historical events and processes to other witnesses of occurrences and personalities in the "world history" of the time. We might say in this regard that that which is hypothetical will always remain so, to a certain degree. Much more complicated and explosive is the question concerning the circumstances of the origin of these biblical writings, their purpose and intent, and the reliability of the detailed events, reports, and documents transmitted. The evaluation of all the biblical writings is made more difficult by the generally accepted view that small, easily examined, and limited narrative and textual units were combined into larger works. More precisely, it is said that older material, stemming from oral formation and tradition, had gone through redaction and had been given new meaning and significance in the larger literary context. In the form of the later redaction, the older material appears as "actualized," or more directly related to the immediacy of the collector and redactor. A view that is always at hand and hard to deny is that in the final form of this work selections were taken from the greater masses of the oral tradition. For that reason, the redaction of the older material occurs in very different ways. At least one example can illustrate that fact.

In the first section of the Old Testament, in the so-called five books of Moses (Pentateuch, in the Greek), older sources have been so closely woven together with later sources that many layers of tradition can be pinpointed, even in a single narrative. Linguistic and factual characteristics make such a source-analysis possible. The Pentateuch begins with a description of the creation of the world and the oldest history of Israel—the stories of the Patriarchs Abraham, Isaac, and Jacob. It ends with the death of Moses at the gates of the Promised Land (Palestine). A historical segment follows, involving the acquiring of the land, up to the Babylonian exile in the sixth century B.C. (books of Joshua through II Kings). In that material, self-contained smaller source fragments are placed next to one another and then woven together to give a plausible, though redactional, historical presentation. A part of this material, along with additions from its own sources, is provided by the so-called historical chronicles (I and II Chronicles). This work tends to offer only the history of the southern kingdom of Judah and thereby emphasizes the significance of Jerusalem, with David playing an appropriately major role. The books of Ezra and Nehemiah set forth postexilic material that cannot with any certainty be reconstructed into a reliable historical picture. And each of these works requires its own method of mastering the subject.

The normal Bible reader who comes to the Book of Books without prejudice, seeking edification and personal enrichment, will be somewhat confused by this talk of so many historical research methods. Must one be aware of all this in order to read the Bible? No! Most of the texts reveal (at times with some difficulty) words and sentences that impress the mind. On the other hand, one cannot avoid the fact that behind many statements there is much "hidden" that should be known in order to understand the details. Modern biblical criticism—

or more exactly, the study of the literary relationships in the biblical writings—began with small observations, which in the course of time stimulated more extensive questions. In the end, the results produced were the same as those outlined above. Nevertheless, the method of critical historical research that began with the Pentateuch will be illustrated further here, in order to empasize the complexity of the historical point of view.

Independent of one another, scholars in eighteenth-century Germany and France noticed the different names for God that were contained in the Hebrew text of the Pentateuch. In one place, the unique name Yahweh would be used, and in another, the more neutral name Elohim (divinity). This distinction made possible the separation of independent strands within the sources. The conclusion was reached that a redactor had joined these strands together in a very artful manner. Beginning with this hypothetical division of sources, modern pentateuchal criticism came into being. Since that time, the study has been refined to a high degree. Nevertheless, its original basic principles still are valid today, even though they have been under attack at times, in spite of better knowledge to the contrary. It has become clear, however, that each of the written sources taken from the Pentateuch has its own emphasis and must be evaluated separately in both historical and theological aspects. The oldest of the writings, which is called the Yahwist (J) because of its primary use of the name Yahweh, was written some time in the early period of the kings (somewhere around 1000 B.C.). Its special emphasis is on the creation story and the history of the Patriarchs, as found in Genesis. Later on, the elements of this layer appear only sporadically. The next layer, which is sometimes debated, is that of the Elohist (E), which prefers the name Elohim for God. This layer had its origin in the middle period of the kings (about the ninth to seventh centuries B.C.). Individual stories of the Patriarchs and the stories of Moses constitute the focal points of this layer. The third stratum is relatively self-contained and is found in the form of Deuteronomy (D). It had its origin in the seventh century B.C. and constituted a type of résumé at the end of the Pentateuch. Before his death, Moses gave a speech to all of Israel, enjoining the people to keep the law of God and confirming the promise of the future possession of the land on both sides of the Jordan. The Priestly Writing (P), without a doubt the youngest of the layers, surrounds the Pentateuch almost as a scaffolding, and its basic elements encompass the first five books of the Bible. It had its origin in the early postexilic period (sixth and fifth centuries B.C.). It has as its focal point genealogical lists and legal matters and for the most part is composed of ritualistic material, from which came its name—Priestly Writings.

If one seeks to visualize these particulars, one will recognize that within the Pentateuch there are at least four rather certain redacted sources—J, E, P, and D. Thus one achieves an impression of the variety within an ancient source, particularly within the Old Testament. In view of the many problems involved, the sources often have been too roughly delimited. The singling out of individual sources from the entire mass of texts, according to their philological and factual points of view, was just the first step. Sine the beginning of this century, a basic step in Old Testament historical critical work involved the attempt to further clarify the circumstances surrounding the origin of the individual sources, J, E, P, and D. This was done partly in order to construct a picture of the development of Israelite religious and intellectual history. One raised questions concerning the oral stage that predated the edited written sources and believed that one was closest to this stage when one discovered individual self-contained pericopes, which may have circulated orally in the same form. The observation that these "small units" were of various kinds led to a research unique in itself—the study of the literary *Gattungen* of the Old Testament. The work of Hermann Gunkel

(1862–1932) pioneered in this area. Gunkel's *Gattung* research expanded into the examination of Old Testament literary forms in general. Today the term *formgeschichtlicher* category pertains to the most essential tasks of Old Testament research. While examining *Gattung* and form in relatively limited units, one did not neglect the study of the editing of the sources into larger units, or ultimately into one great unit, such as the Pentateuch: The principles governing the final redaction should be observed in order to see the whole picture in its proper light. In perspective, this literary work, the Pentateuch, appears to be not so much the product of a single short period of creative activity, but the result of a literary historical process which, in each phase, is open to questions concerning its historical difficulties and backgrounds.

One can classify the understanding of this whole literary process under the history of the transmission of the Pentateuch. Whereas *Gattung* criticism and form criticism limit themselves to small units which presumably already were fashioned in their oral form, tradition criticism and redaction criticism have their orientation in the written records of this literature, available to us as an end product. Next we find textual criticism, which is concerned with the nature of the entire text, as manifested in many different manuscripts and translations. In difficult cases, the text becomes clear only through a comparison of these various versions. Strictly speaking, this clearly defined extensive division of the sources is the groundwork which must be done for historical research. Only when a statement is viewed in reference to its age, its locality, its formal use, or its intended purpose, can the historian create the combinations of material needed for the reconstruction of a historical course of events. That may sound difficult, but it corresponds to the complexity we discover in the study of sources—at least that is true of the Old Testament.

One certainly must admit that not every source that comes to us from antiquity needs to be subjected to such an extensive method of research. However, not every ancient written source had such a complex history of transmission as did the biblical writings, which not only went through a constant process of growth but, in the form in which we have them, also experienced a type of selection process. The selection took place from the ongoing tradition, in order to preserve for all time in a valid and final canonical form, that which was thought to be fruitful and effective. Modern historians can study the limits and possibilities of historical expression and the way it was used by viewing the significance of the inclusion and editing of historical facts, narratives, tradition, and the manner of transmission in the various periods. The criterion for source criticism is related to the total process of scientific historical research and at least can be helpful in testing a sentence such as the following: "From a scientific-theoretical point of view, the postulate of being 'value free' is self evident" (J. Habermas) [11:86]. When one looks at the material of ancient sources, it is very obvious that every expression carries with it some intrinsic value of its time, and it is just that value that makes the statement worthy of transmission, historically binding, and for that reason, of use to scientific historical research. The postulate of being "value free" is a self-deceptive thing in historical research because no period of time can be separated from the values that influence and determine it. One finds it quite difficult to isolate the concept of values of some past period of time from the sources. To put it in a more banal way: The statement that "in every age, people have eaten" involves a conclusion containing no historical value. However, what people ate and how people ate are questions of very great historical interest. To place this on a higher level, one could say that a historical statement is not determined by the "fact that something happened, but rather by the way the event was valued—what it was worth, what was contributed by it—the kind of information "transmitted" to us. This direction of questioning attains a validity for historical research that goes beyond the mere gathering of facts.

The differentiation of the pentateuchal sources and those of the other Old Testament books, however, has been carried so far that it has caused the Bible to be viewed as meaningless by many naïve critics. These books were not put together with scissors and paste. Such critics overlook the marked process of growth in the literature, which was not accomplished simply by an editor behind a desk, but grew out of the worldly and religious narratives, recitations, and traditions, in order that it might live on in some set form for ritual purposes. This literary- and form-critical process of the Holy Scriptures follows its own laws.

It goes without saying that it was on the basis of insights drawn from the science of literature and in connection with precise source-critical studies, that presentations of the history of Israel and of the theology of the Old Testament were written. The principles of these methods have been expanded into the area of New Testament studies. However, since New Testament studies are not concerned with the collection of various works on which man labored for hundreds of years, but rather with work that was done in a few decades, other methods and criteria are to be used. We will discuss that topic later.

In summary, it may be said that historical research must weigh every testimony, every statement, every piece of writing, every object, as a legitimate means of discovering knowledge. However, in view of such details, one can come to further insights only if one places those objects and those testimonies from the sources in the context of their own respective time and location wherever possible. For the very essence of historical research does not involve the task of establishing the existence or factuality of an event, but rather of clarifying and presenting the way it happened, or the presuppositions behind it, of which the transmitted material speaks.

II. Portrayal and Hermeneutic of History

a. Principal Considerations

The knowledge that has been gained from the written sources and other materials left to us from the past makes it possible to bring together greater combinations of materials, in the course of ever larger periods of time. Therefore we can create history (*Geschichte*) on the basis of historical (*historischen*) knowledge. By necessity, if the writer of history desires to be more than just a chronicler or recorder who registers facts, dates, and events, that writer must take on the work of connecting with his or her own words the individual results achieved through research. Therefore the portrayal of history opens up an extensive field for responsible interaction with the sources and with their use. For it is obvious that the comprehensive presentation of individual incidents never can deviate from the insights of individual research, but in most cases it does. Therein we find that the special task of the historian is not just to transmit statistics, including facts and events, but to formulate a picture of the past that is understandable because it has been simplified. That picture is gleaned from reflection on the complex material that has been transmitted. The historical picture thus transmitted leaves its imprint on the reader, or should leave its imprint, and therefore unconsciously becomes the foundation for a "historical consciousness." This necessary simplification within the framework of history portrayal does not always fully express the results of extensive historical research. Since every form of presentation has its limitations, here we will treat the portrayal of history in its limited relationship to the hermeneutic of history. Hermeneutic is understood as the attempt to reconstruct the event, not only in its supposed actuality, but to make the course of historical events understandable and comprehensible for posterity. This means that in the presentation of an event, the judgment of the one who is presenting is also involved. To that extent, hermeneutic works with the independent value-categories of every age in order that through them, the value-conceptions of the past can be made visible and understandable. The ongoing question of interpretation of history, in the sense of a certain order that holds the past events together or influences them, can be answered by hermeneutic, but is in actuality the task of the philosophy of history. Strictly speaking, the hermeneutic of history should limit itself to the translation of the past into present ways of understanding, a task which is difficult in itself. In this way the significant question that stands above all others is forced upon us and is combined with the business of presenting and transmitting that is involved in the portrayal of history. It should not be the task of every portrayal to intensify the hermeneutical process of transforming the past into forms of present understanding, right up to the last significant question.

The task and privilege of describing history—attributing a higher meaning and significance to past events—often is interwoven with the enthusiasm of the author, who becomes or feels it necessary to become that force which gives form to the past—a process made possible only through reflection. Let us look once again at the examples given in the beginning of this book.

Kaemmel's description of the battle of Königgrätz can rely, in every detail, upon validated reports. The way in which he presents it is very artful; moreover, he makes use of very impressive scenic images. In saying that, we have said quite a lot. The details are so tersely brought together that the reader is swept along—from the difficulty of the battle, to the anxiety concerning the outcome, to the defeated army with all its casualties, and on to the jubilation of the victorious army. The participation of the narrator in that description is evident in the eyewitness portrayal of the Austrian rout ("as wild animals before a forest fire") or just as evident in the words concerning the "strong stand" taken by his own Saxon countrymen. Great stress is placed on the meeting of the victorious Prussian king with the crown prince, who had been a very decisive factor in the battle. This emphasis is due primarily to the fact that, since that time, the founding of the Reich had brought the Saxons under the rule of the Prussians. Looking back on those events, the attitude of the victors at Königgrätz seems very fitting.

In spite of the somewhat plastic urgency, this Saxon account remains to a certain degree cool and distant—reserved in all evaluations of accomplishments and registering in a very painful way the losses on both sides. Anecdotes containing details are not evident. The cigar scene between Bismarck and Moltke, although well attested (it has even been captured in a painting by C. Röchling), found its strongest response in Prussia. Thus we honor our heroes. One German textbook of 1939 utilized this heroism in the service of ideological purposes. There we find the following description of the events at Königgrätz: "The king halted on a hill; next to him was Bismarck on his huge chestnut horse, sitting tall in the saddle, dressed in a grey mantle, his large gleaming eyes looking out from beneath his helmet—just like a giant out of the old Nordic time" [7:153].

The mixing of direct discourse into an account is a special problem, undergirded in part by validated information and in part by the fantasy of the author. Hence, in the textbook, the author has the worried king ask Moltke, "If there should be a retreat, what will be the outcome?" Moltke: "There will be no retreat. Prussia's future is at stake. Today your majesty will win not just the battle but the whole campaign." Only the second part sounds as though it might be in Moltke's own words. Jahnke's book on Bismarck phrases it just a bit differently:

" 'Today your majesty has won not just the battle but the whole campaign,' said Moltke late that evening as he rode with the king over the battlefield toward Horicz."

These quotations certainly were taken from a folklike didactic literature, because they have a broader effect than does serious analysis. They leave their mark on the general historical consciousness. The paintings of the period accomplish the same service by depicting great "ideal typical" scenes. The best-known example is the *Proclamation of the Kaiser*. The painter Anton von Werner once was expressly summoned to the crown prince by a telegram: "His royal majesty wants you to know that you will find something here worthy to paint if you will appear here before January 18" [9:668]. Much to his surprise, von Werner was not taken to the battlefield at Paris, but was led into the Hall of Mirrors at Versailles. Few people know that there are two versions of the famous painting. One places the Kaiser behind the podium in the center, whereas the other—the more famous—places Bismark in his white uniform at the center with the great men of the coming Reich around him. Thus we find historical presentation and interpretation together in the same painting. What is historical? No photograph exists and no eyewitnesses have left their reports. The brush of Anton von Werner gave testimony to history in the way it was seen by that artist. Here we have not played down the fact that policies in regard to the principles of historical portrayal of this kind have not changed. Totalitarian systems, especially those authoritarian systems oriented to the left, brought forth and continue to bring forth a flood of pictures, which seek in their placative earnestness to portray the ideological purposes of a state's leadership or to see their prior history confirmed through the portrayal of revolutionary and other scenes. Wherever necessary, such scenes are adjusted (the raising of the red flag on the Berlin Reichstag in 1945) or rearranged (the coming together of the two political blocs, KPD and SPD, into the SED in East Berlin in the year

1945). The portrayal of history is often intensified for well-known and intentional symbolism. Such procedures may be termed illegitimate. But who can write a law for human dealings? Actually, the symbolic concentration of entire chains of events into one single chain is one of the oldest means of presenting historical actions. One might remember the unusually large pharaoh figures on the walls of the Egyptian temples. They are depicted in battle, with the enemy in a cowering position, totally suppressed and defeated. In the middle of the scene is the chariot of the pharaoh, bearing the victorious divine king. Small forts around the edge, decorated with names, suggest a map. The symbolically immense pharaoh is not just anywhere in the picture, but in the middle of the cities and fortresses of these foreign lands. The victor at that time was not represented as smoking a good cigar. In contrast to such sublime respectability, one is more likely to see the pharaoh with an uplifted club in his hand. In his left hand he holds a group of prisoners by their hair, and he is striking their heads. That is the gesture of a victor!

b. The Oldest Forms of Portrayal in the Old Testament

Old Israel left us no pictorial representation of its history. The Assyrian palace reliefs contain a few scenes from Israel's history, but they are conceptualized from the point of view of the victor. However, songs of victory are among the oldest material found in Old Testament sources. These are hymns or songs from the crisis points of Jewish history—from the decisive hours of their existence and are sung by women. After the rescue at the Red Sea, shortly after the Exodus from Egypt, Miriam sang this song recorded in Exodus 15:21:

> Sing to the Lord, for he has triumphed gloriously;
> The horse and his rider he has thrown into the sea.

The motif which runs throughout Israelite history appears here very emphatically. The deliverer is the Lord, and no one else. It was not some ideological varnish, or some obsequious gratefulness, or some quiet fear that brought this expression to the singer's lips, but rather the unavoidable and undeniable conviction that God was there with them; that he had delivered them; that he had destroyed the threat to them.

The song of Miriam may be a mere fragment. In contrast, the song of Deborah (Judg. 5) has been retained in all its fullness. Its difficult and, in part, corrupted text gives the greatest indication of being quite old and authentic to that period of time—that period shortly after the taking of the land by the Israelite tribes (c. 1100 B.C.). A few of those tribes resided on the great plain Jezreel, which stretched south of old Galilee to the heights of present day Haifa, and they were threatened by a strong coalition of Canaanite princes. The battle took place on the plain near the Kishon brook. Israel's chances were practically nil. The ill-equipped Jews stood against an enemy power fitted out with chariots. Then Deborah sang:

> Lord, when thou didst go forth from Seir,
>   when thou didst march from the region of Edom,
> the earth trembled,
>   and the heavens dropped,
>   yea, the clouds dropped water.
> The mountains quaked before the Lord.

In actuality, the rain must have softened the earth on the plain so that the wheels of the enemy's chariots became stuck in the mud. After the great response on Israel's side to the challenge, demonstrating their great courage and willingness to fight, the battle began—a battle employing cosmic measures:

> From heaven fought the stars,
>   from their courses they fought against Sisera [the enemy's
>   general]

> The torrent Kishon swept them away,
>   the onrushing torrent, the torrent Kishon.

There is no lack of anecdotal detail. Sisera fled the battlefield and was taken into Jael's tent, after he had asked her for water. She offered him milk and cream, but at the same time reached for the tent peg and then pounded it into his head. This bloody scene did not satisfy the author. He depicted Sisera's mother waiting at home for the victorious king. In her anguished uncertainty, she was comforted by the noble women at her side. She inspired them all with her strong wishes:

> Are they not finding and dividing the spoil?—
>   A maiden or two for every man;
> spoil of dyed stuffs for Sisera,
>   spoil of dyed stuffs embroidered,
>   two pieces of dyed work embroidered for my neck as spoil?

In the midst of the noise of these women's voices, the author thundered his final chord:

> So perish all thine enemies, O Lord!
>   But thy friends be like the sun as he rises in his might.

Long before Homer, the song of Deborah was a creation of the highest poetic power and descriptive maturity. For that dramatic conclusion is masterfully constructed: It reports the death of the defeated general, not on the battlefield, but on his way home, at the hands of a woman, and does not emphasize the effect of Sisera's death, but stresses only the women waiting for him to come home. It shows the great empathy of the author. A bit of history is transmitted but it is composed so dramatically in its narrow confines, and its quick changes of scenery create such great stress that the grand conclusion of the poem takes on the quality of a striking hymn to the true victors. The God of Israel has granted his people the victory. The

enemy of Israel becomes also the enemy of God. The
unexpected has taken place; the heavens helped those who
were at a technical disadvantage, not through irrational
miraculous deeds, but through highly practical use of the land
and the rain of a cloudburst, which caused the Kishon to rise
and flood the battlefield. The actual wonder is that this flooding
happened at exactly the right time. The land, rain, and other
circumstances might lead us to a rationalistic explanation.
However, because it occurred at the decisive hour, it became
an empirical experience of God. Following the mass scenes and
the clamor of battle, the author finally succeeds in directing our
attention to personalities; and in their defeat and misfortune,
the cause and extent of the achievement becomes clear. The
concluding hymn is not merely expression of proud triumph
over the weakness of the opponent, but is both a thanksgiving
and the humble recognition of victory over an apparently
invincible coalition.

The Old Testament portrayal of history has various
expressions of such picturesque earnestness. In the battle
against the Amalekites in Exodus 17, Israel was victorious as
long as Moses held his hands up. In fact, his hands had to be
supported until the enemy could be defeated. Later, as Israel
prepared to cross the Jordan and could see the fortress of
Jericho across the way, spies were sent out to bring back news
of the land. They were taken in by a prostitute who lived in a
house on the city wall. The woman spoke about the way the
land shook before the onmarching Israelites. Later she placed a
red cord in her window so that she presumably might be spared
by the approaching tribes of Israel. More probably, the cord
was a sign indicating where access to the city might be found.
The involvement of prostitutes in the conquering of enemy
cities is a theme found in much literature, including the
classical Greek. In Joshua 2, the woman who received the spies
is viewed as a tool of God who gave the Israelites courage and
who probably was active in making the defeat of the city

possible. The anecdotal detail found in complexes of old narrative units, often with almost legendary aspects was always built into and motivated larger historical movements, as in the time of Moses and the Patriarchs and served to convince the people that God was leading them. He always found ways and means for bringing his promises to fulfillment. We are at all times in the presence of true historical remembrance, and nowhere is the historically concrete dissolved into abstract thought-forms. The biblical writer connected his narrative to the hermeneutical goal, showing the constant way of God with his people, in the midst of the fear and hesitation of all the concerned groups. In the empirical experience and through it all, the historically active rule of God is made perceivable.

In view of such means of representation, one can judge that the modern historian has a difficult time with the early history of Israel. From the treasures of old narrative traditions and their complex editing, he or she must recognize their total coloring by theology and determine what actually happened, for there were causes which gave birth to these traditions and reasons which, in turn, led to their formation and transmission. Israel's oldest history appears in forms rich in detailed knowledge which attests to the impact of real events. Of course there are subtle distinctions in this regard, from source to source.

Nowhere does there exist such distance between historical impulse and poetic freedom as that found, for example, in the great classic epics of Homer and Virgil. That fact must be stressed. For those writers were free to allow their heroes to become what they are to us today—heroes with their own strengths and personal goals, even though they are ensnarled in the heavenly world where the gods sometime help, but sometimes bring misfortune. One cannot compare Odysseus and Moses. Odysseus, cloaked in legend, stands alone and acts for himself. In contrast, Moses is a man called of God, who desires to do nothing for himself; he cannot act alone and is closely tied to his people and to his God. At times he was reluctant; at other times, severely tested; and at all times, at one with the destiny of his people. Miracles of food in the desert may have helped the Israelites along their way, but only added to the impression that the journey was filled with misery. The producing of food and water was always empirically related to definite factors in the southern desert of Palestine and the Sinai.

Therefore it is wrong to associate the historical traditions of Israel with the concept of myth. Where God speaks to man, there can be no myth. Divine discourse is the representative means of linking historical experience with questions of existence. At no time was Israel subjected to the whims of its God or to the revenge of the gods, as were Odysseus and his followers. In Israel's history, God's will was expressed in other ways—in his preserving and redeeming strength in spite of all the errors of humanity. One might term that the hermeneutic of history and might perceive within it the attempt to reveal the way of God for himself and for those yet to come. It is, though, the understanding and presentation of history which is founded in empiricism—and the experience of God is an essential part of that empiricism. In the Old Testament, God is not just a "thought"; rather he is "experienced." In the history of Israel, there is nothing to demythologize, because there is no myth; instead, one finds an interpreted concrete event. Demythologizing, therefore, can never be effective in the Old Testament —*entmythisierung* might be a better word than the non-word *entmythologisierung)* because there was no cause or reason for it. It may be that in due time, someone may create a special concept of myth. Later the same question will be addressed to the New Testament and to its transmission. If Israel had viewed its oldest history as myth, it never would have realized the continuity of its faith affirmation that saw it through so many catastrophes. It cannot be denied that the Old Testament assimilates myths in some places. But the sources of these myths were not in Israel—they came from outside, and Israel transformed them and subjected their contents to the rule of their own God. Often these myths were shortened for polemical reasons and became quite foreign to their roots—placed in another thought-world altogether.

c. The Period of the Kings of Israel and Judah

The method of presenting history varies from place to place in the Old Testament. In the earlier narratives centering around the Patriarchs—Moses and the heroic leaders and fighters of the period of the taking of the land, such as Gideon (Judg. 6–8) and the strong man Sampson (Judg. 13-16)—we perceive traces of old legends. In the most direct sense of the word they are encountered as spoken, declared, or oral tradition. With the beginning of the period of the kings, the source material was altered. The developing state created institutions that were interested in recording and noting the events that took place in that period. Over and over again the books of the Old Testament mention the chronicles of the kings of Israel and Judah. Unfortunately, we no longer possess these writings except for fragments or large segments which have been incorporated into the Old Testament. The presentation of Saul's reign, the rule of David, and to a certain degree that of his successor, Solomon, as found in the books of Samuel and Kings, contain much desired detail. They are unusually rich and highly developed writings, which demonstrate exact observation and a great sense of the art of presentation. Eduard Meyer (1855–1930) heaped great praise upon these works. In his *History of Antiquity,* he wrote:

> The narrator shows a very intimate knowledge of the events of the period of David and Solomon. He must have been very close to the inner circle. Because of this, every political and apologetic

tendency is missing. With cool objectivity, but with an unsurpassed irony, the narrator observed the events, and for this reason, his report is unequalled in its clearness. This record is far removed from religious coloring or any thought of supernatural leadership. The course of the world and the retribution which takes place in the chain of events brought about by one's own guilt are themes presented in full relevance, even as they appeared to the observer.

The golden age of the Jewish monarchy gave birth to real history writing. No other culture of the ancient Orient was able to accomplish that. Even the Greeks did not reach that accomplishment until the height of their development in the fifth century and then immediately went on beyond it. Here we are dealing, in contrast, with a people who were just developing their culture. The elements of their culture, such as an easily learned script, they, like the Greeks, had taken over from older civilizations. This makes their own accomplishments even more astounding. We stand here, as in all of history, before the riddle that cannot be explained—that of innate gifts [42:285/6].

These words of Eduard Meyer have been frequently quoted, as well as contested. In fact, they must be critiqued, in particular, in regard to the normative validity attributed unreservedly to Greek historical writing. One must always ask why Meyer was so carried away in his unusually high evaluation of Old Testament historical writing and what prompted him to speak of "real historical writing."

The decisive factor for Meyer was the observation that the reports concerning David's reign were oriented not only to persons and to their stories but also contained overlapping relationships and pinpointed historical problems. The persons described were not presented for their self-willed deeds, but acted under the impulse of circumstances and obligations and often fit into an almost dramatic flow of events. They both confronted and withstood those events. This is most clearly seen in the burning question concerning which of David's sons should or could become his successor. Usually one refers to the complex of chapters found in II Samuel 7 through 20, with the addition of I Kings 1:1–2:11, when one seeks to know more about the history of the successor to David's throne. Indeed, these texts read as one interrelated account, beginning in a programmatic way in II Samuel 7, with a divine announcement from the prophet Nathan. David will establish a "house," meaning that he will found a dynasty that will be long lasting. Only in a peripheral way is it noted that this divine pronouncement is the germinal element for the later so-called "messianic expectation." The essence of that expectation was that an ideal ruler from the tribe of David would appear. The dynastic kingdom of the Davidic rulers in Jerusalem was the decisive presupposition for this. The further course of the history of David shows, however, that this divine promise seemed to be threatened by human guilt and tragic errors. For the sons of David, who were the frontrunners to succeed to the throne, were of a very different nature from their father. Thus David did not rush to decide the question of successor—one who would see to the continuation of his extensive federation of tribes. As far as we can determine the history of the sons, there were three who could and actually did lay claim to the throne. We will list them according to their age—Amnon, Absalom, and Adonijah. The oldest, Ammon, was slain by Absalom as a consequence of some private affair. Severe discord betwen Absalom and his father then brought about a cunningly contrived rebellion which almost succeeded in giving Absalom the throne during David's lifetime.

The rebellion of Absalom, as it traditionally has been called, is among the most masterfully composed historical presentations of the Davidic period. The preparation, the actual course of events, and the macabre conclusion are clearly described. David was very clever in fleeing Jerusalem and leaving the capital to his surprised son. Absalom was not equal to the situation and, in the confusion of the first hours, was open to good advice, but followed bad. He risked an immediate attack upon the king and his devoted and experienced army. He had just taken over Jerusalem but was extremely insecure in that new position. He left the capital, followed the king across the Jordan, and paid for his foolhardiness with his life. Personal misfortune was to blame: He caught his hair in the branches of a tree, and his horse ran from under him. Defenseless, he was quickly pierced by an opponent's weapon. With the leader of the resistance dead, David became more firm in his power than ever and returned to Jerusalem.

The way leading to the throne now seemed free for Adonijah, the third potential candidate, who arranged some insurance for his position by winning over the leading men in the army and the priesthood—a very proper group. However, his intrigues were countered by another group who supported the king and had their own plans. Taking advantage of the new situation in a very clever way, the prophet Nathan sent the woman Bathsheba, whom the king once had loved passionately, to David to plead the cause of Solomon, who enjoyed the protection of Nathan's group. On behalf of Nathan, Bathsheba questioned the king concerning whether he had designated his son Adonijah to inherit the throne, since Adonijah was at the point of having himself declared king. Full of impatience, Nathan did not even wait until the end of this conversation to barge into the king's chambers and press him for a decision. He declared that Adonijah had given a feast and had not invited him, Nathan, or any of his group. Did David command that kind of thing? Who wanted to exclude them? The aging king was taken by surprise, and Nathan left the chambers, having gained the thing he desired—David, under oath, had declared Solomon, son of Bathsheba, as his successor. The ceremony of anointing was at once carried out by Nathan and his party. As a result, the surprised Adonijah was automatically designated as the usurper and was forced to seek asylum—his life was in danger.

This dramatic course of events in the narrator's presentation was the very thing that Meyer had in mind when he used the words, "an intimate knowledge of the events at court." But did Meyer not err in using such phrases as "real historical writing," "every political and apologetic tendency is missing," "the narrator observed the events with cool objectivity," and "he viewed all events with unsurpassed irony"? It is certain that the narrator described the "chain of events," but was he really far removed "from religious coloring or any thought of supernatural leadership"? Indeed, what Meyer meant was that this was a form of historical presentaion that did not push God forward as the model regent, but recognized the inner compulsion within the events themselves. It perceived that the living out of passions creates necessary conflicts which in turn do not deny moves such as those made by Nathan, or other political maneuvering. The picture of a secular struggle for power which makes use of inner political structures and the favor of the hour looms very realistically before the eyes of the readers.

So far, so good. However, the biblical author is deeply convinced that in the midst of this obviously human and political course of action, God is present and at work, and that all these forces become the tools of God—especially in view of the moment of dramatic decision. Quite often he says that very thing. When Absalom was faced with the question of whether to wait or to pursue David immediately, he listened to questionable advice and set out in great haste after his father's army. The biblical writer said at that point, "For the Lord had ordained to defeat the good counsel of Ahithophel, so that the Lord might bring evil upon Absalom" (II Sam. 17:14). In this side remark, the author gives a clear indication that at the very height of the battle, one can see the real force at work behind the obviously secular course of events. The narrator makes his judgment at this point on the basis of a clear theological perspective. The fact that this remark falls exactly at the point of culmination in the story of Absalom points to the masterful construction of this form of writing. In contrast to Meyer, one ought not to speak here of "real historical writing," but rather of a tendentious style of narration, or one that serves a purpose whose goal is clear: David is justified; his rule is cloaked with the glow of divine providence. Thus the power of a ruling house is supported, a result that the narrator desired. "Court literature, colored by a distinct bias," and perhaps edited by the hand of a priest, is the very least one could say in evaluating these biblical stories, or narratives.

However, such a judgment would not perceive that even modern historical presentation is no different in principle. If it is to be understood, it too must be regarded as tendentious and eclectic. This can be seen in the study of the Greek fathers of historical writing, Herodotus and Thucydides, and their interaction with the sources. Tacitus was very conscious of the danger of a subjective treatment of the sources, as he attempted to write *sina ira et studio,* without ever being true to his goal. It is part of the essence of every historical presentation that it must be influenced by the point of view of its author, which necessarily gives the impression of a certain bias, or prejudice. In this connection, however, it should not be forgotten that "positions" and prejudices can be, and as a rule, actually are effective in themselves as determining factors in the course of history. Thus they must never be overlooked: Historical research always must pinpoint them and historical presentation always must seek to portray them. What the later researcher may consider as "cool objectivity" and "unsurpassed irony" in the study of the historical relationships in his sources, needs to be viewed in the greater relationship of his own presuppositions and the intellectual situation of his own time and made the object of hidden possibilities and potential.

The writer of history, as one who regulates, must not try to grasp all the potential factors at one time, but must be content to establish a few matters that will bear out the facts. He is equipped only with language as a means of expression. It is a characteristic of human speech that it can only describe in sequence those complex courses of events that are happening at the same time and under the control of the same active power. To be sure, the author will always have before his eyes the entire historical course or process, but he can unfold the entire picture only gradually. He must follow the law of logical sequence of presentation. He often must only hint at, anticipate, and refer back, but finally can only hope that the weight of his presentation has conveyed the whole intended picture to the reader in a convincing and complete enough way. To that extent, all historical presentation is inseparable from hermeneutic, for all active events that are linguistically and logically perceived are actively influenced by the interpretative and receptive understanding of the interpreter. Every attempt to make something understandable is basically a hermeneutical procedure.

A probing of our biblical example might produce a "contrasting view" of the Davidic period that we do not possess, but this cannot be found by searching behind the text for opposing tendencies that might convey another picture of the period. It would be difficult to go beyond hypotheses, and it is obvious that it would be hard to reduce a historical presentation that has emerged from many points of view to one that is value-free in nature. One also could not make such a reduction serve some other concept of history, or set it forth as the only valid opinion. To be sure, critical analysis of the sources will involve, to some degree, the consideration of other ways of understanding a motive or course of action, but without demanding that the discovery be viewed in all certainty as irrefutable "historical truth." Indeed only the poet and the writer have the freedom to make use of persons, events, circumstances, and motifs in service of their own concepts. Biblical novels, as effective as they may be, have little to do with history—just as little as the freedom of the interpreting art. *The King David Report*, a book by the modern author Stefan Heym, makes use of the material outlined here and then promptly goes off in another direction. In that novel, Solomon is represented as one who suppressed truth, but in reality, as successor to David, he was the one who finally allowed it to win full expression. With Solomon's succession, the work of David was truly recognized as having laid the foundation for the major power status for Israel-Judah. There is nothing that would cause us to think that Solomon sought to ascribe that success to himself or that he wanted to hide it.

It is remarkable that in the other great historical work of the Old Testament—the work of chronicles found mainly in I and II Chronicles—David is elevated at the expense of Solomon and is celebrated as the actual founder of the temple cult. It shows that postexilic Israel undertook to rearrange the strong points of its own earlier history and to reshape them hermeneutically to conform to a changed situation and intellectual climate. The author of the chronicles (at the latest, third century B.C.) sought to strengthen the highly powerful significance of the temple and its cult by pronouncing David to be the father of the organization surrounding the temple in Jerusalem. He was clothed with messianic hope and viewed as the founder of a dynasty, and at the same time, was given credit for drawing up the plans for the building of the temple. Solomon appears in the role of one who carried out the plans of his father. Without a doubt this was a reinterpretation of history and also the development of another "historical picture" based on contemporary conditions and necessities. In the views of this later period, Solomon could not appear as the protector of the temple cult because he was too well known for his worldliness and his selfishness at court. David had brought entirely different presuppositions to the task, and these allowed him to assume a more extensive position of value. He was the conqueror of Jerusalem, guarantor of the dynasty, and not least of all, the author to which many of the psalms were ascribed, and thus one who prepared the way for the sacramental functions and orders at the Jerusalem Temple.

It would be instructive to cite further examples of Israelite historical writing, in order to deepen, enrich, or modify the criteria and observations brought forward. Much material is found in the unfolding tradition around the great prophet Elijah (the first half of ninth century B.C.) in the northern kingdom of Israel, as well as about his student and successor Elisha. Their work extended into the period of Jehu, who under turbulent circumstances won the throne in Jezreel and Samaria and launched a dynasty for the northern state of Israel, apart from that of David in Jerusalem. The study of this circle of tradition can be found in I Kings 17 through II Kings 10, with the exception of a few interspersed passages containing special material. Such study is very rewarding because one can distinguish numerous layers of the traditional forms—from the very earliest legends, up to the description of well-thought-out tactics of political revolution. One supersedes the other. The very laws and peculiarities of the ongoing formation of legends and the transmission of motifs can be seen by comparing the Elijah narratives with those about Elisha. For the first time, one catches sight of the extensive effects of prophecy and its tradition in Israel. In the complexity of the situation, one can see the influences of the prophets on the social and religious life of their land. One need only remember the well-known presentations of God's judgment on top of Mount Carmel (I Kings 18) and the annexation of Naboth's vineyard (I Kings 21). Second Kings 17 takes on its own independent significance in its attempt to give a historical summary after the fall of the northern kingdom in 722-21 B.C. This is true also of II Kings 22-23, which is concerned with the so-called reform of Josiah, which sought to bring about an extensive and comprehensively planned new ordering of the state and temple cult, in view of the diminishing Assyrian influence on Israel and Judah. If we are viewing the course of events correctly, then we must see Josiah removing the Assyrian cult step by step, before he brought the other Israelite holy places in the land under immediate control of the Jerusalem temple, to which he gave a monopoly position. The last step was taken in 622 B.C. and was very successful, since the postexilic community now could think of itself as related almost without interruption to Jerusalem and the temple cult. The messianic expectations of the ancient stories of the kings were focused there. The continuation of Jerusalem guaranteed the continuation of the people of God and thus became a symbol.

With these observations, we have painted the broad horizons of the way in which old Israel began to understand itself; these point far beyond its beginning in the period of David and Solomon and gradually help to interpret Israel's role in the international structures of that time. The most decisive contribution in understanding the conflict between Israel and the great powers since the ninth century B.C., or at the latest, since the eighth century, is rendered by the prophets (after the second century, by the apocalyptists). In the eighth and ninth centuries, the great powers were Assyria and Babylon; after the sixth century, the Persians; and finally the Greeks.

d. The Contribution of the Prophets

The prophets were not writers of history, but they reacted to the events of their time, and for this reason they afford inestimable material that cannot be overlooked in gaining historical knowledge and understanding of that period. This material can lay claim to high authenticity, but of course we should understand that the book of a prophet transmitted to us should not be fully attributed to the man whose name is on its cover. These prophetic books have been added to, enriched, and edited in complex ways—the whole process of their transmission is an independent field of research. Yet there are numerous references to historical events, circumstances, failures, and expectations that make it possible to arrange the historical situations of the individual narratives within the transmitted books in some kind of order. There is no doubt that the oldest complete prophetic book is that of Amos, a prophet who began his work in the middle of the eighth century B.C. in the northern kingdom of Israel at the time of Jeroboam II. Isaiah was called to be a prophet in Jerusalem in the year that King Uzziah died, perhaps at the beginning of the thirties of the eighth century. He experienced the great Assyrian attack of 701 on Judah and its capital. Exactly one hundred years later, Jeremiah carried on his activity. He was present at the fall of Jerusalem (587–76) and finally was carried off to Egypt. His contemporary in the Babylonian exile was Ezekiel. He had been deported to Babylon in 597 B.C. We can assign some dates to certain points in his life.

The days of the Exile are most difficult to pinpoint. The prophet of the period is unknown and has been called the second Isaiah (due to our quandary), because his writings are found in the last part of the Book of Isaiah (chap. 40–55). He carried on his work in Babylon and made mention of the Persian king, Cyrus II (559–529 B.C.). The last prophets who can be clearly assigned a date are Haggai and Zechariah. They were active during the reign of Darius I, Hystaspis (522–486 B.C.), the Persian king to whom Jerusalem was subject at that time and who was later drawn into world history in the course of the Ionian rebellion, when he lost the battle of Marathon (490 B.C.). The prophets Haggai and Zechariah struggled from the fall of 520 to the spring of 519 in rebuilding the temple, which actually was dedicated in the year 515 B.C. Thus one can sketch the temporal framework for the appearances of Israel's prophets. In such limited space it is difficult to deal with the total effect of the prophets upon the historical consciousness of Israel and upon the people's understanding of historical movements. As we have said, the prophets were not writers of history; however, they did sharpen their contemporaries' awareness of external as well as internal politics, social life, religious life, and cultic life.

They taught that all these should be understood as interrelated. For this reason, the prophets are correctly viewed as the true interpreters of historical events in the Old Testament.

The "historical consideration" of the prophets is primarily existential, insofar as the prophet takes his stance in an immediate encounter with a decisive hour—that moment at which he was encountered by the divine word—the hour when he had been certain that he must proclaim his word in a given situation. He was under a compulsion to share this certainty because he was convinced that he had been divinely appointed to speak. For that reason, the details of the historical hour, conditioned by time, were incorporated into the prophecy, not for the prophet's own satisfaction, but to explain God's demands both then and now, the warnings, and what the prophet has to share concerning the false evaluation of the hour. The word was often spoken to a group little disposed to accept it; yet its intention was to explain, clarify, admonish, and warn. By necessity, the prophet included possible future consequences. Why this certainty of the future was always expressed in negative terms is a question that cannot be answered briefly. For the prophet himself vacillated in his judgments and recognized, in spite of some message of doom, an unquenchable feeling of hope—a hope that could be clothed in a passionate intercession for his people (Amos 7:1-6). Isaiah, in spite of his mission to make his people even more stiff-necked and thereby ripe for destruction (6:9-12), considered the possibility of a historical turn of events (7:1-17) and spoke of it clearly (8:23–9:6).

From this observation of prophetic activity, we discover two dimensions of their sphere of perception. The first is the present, which is challenged, and the second is the future, which is the focal point for addressing the present. There is also a third dimension—the past. For it is against that background that the prophetic discourse is unfolded. If it is believable, it achieves a place in the continuum of the tradition of faith and history of Israel. As an example, Amos 3:2 should be remembered. It contains a phrase that serves as a basic paradigm for all the prophetic discourse of Israel.

> You only have I known of all the families of the earth;
> therefore I will punish you for all your iniquities.

God's choosing of Israel, a fact that was fully and visibly present in the Patriarchs and in the deliverance from Egypt, appeared to the Israelites as the pledge of the past, which possessed full validity and certainty as a guarantee of survival for all time. Now the prophet directs his attention to that untouchable, highly esteemed possession and draws an opposite conclusion concerning the "chosen nation" status. Israel's privilege of being chosen from all the peoples of the earth and lifted above all of them would bring about a related opposing force. The highly touted state of being chosen stands over against a great fall, which would be brought about by the mass of Israel's obvious failures.

Prophetic discourse thrives on the knowledge of the traditions and obligations which the past places upon a people. However, in view of the corruption of the present, it knows how to describe consequences for the future that are rooted in inevitable failures, over against obligations. For the historical consciousness of Israel, these prophetic realms of conception are related to the strongest elements of its own thought and hope. The knowledge of God's provision for and guidance of Israel's early existence in Palestine was amplified to become a manifestation of God's will for salvation and deliverance. Israel's history was oriented in God's will for deliverance, which had been historically manifested in its history and was thus visible, provable, and demonstrable. Israel's conviction—its faith in God—was anchored firmly in God's salvific will. From that faith, Israel projected itself beyond the catastrophes of the present to the promised salvation of God in some near or distant future. In their own destiny, the Israelites could see the way God was dealing with them in spite of all their failures. The relationship between these three dimensions, which, without much reflection, we have designated as past/present/future did not possess an abstract character for Israel, but was filled with firm conceptions of a living relationship between God and itself which already was in progress and would continue to be so. The past meant promise, but also iniquity. The future meant judgment, but also fulfillment of the promises. But these are not just abstractions; they are conceptions that shall clarify the unfamiliar to our own consciousness. Deutero-Isaiah developed forms of thought and speech designed to confirm those things that had just been contemplated. In Isaiah 40:1-2, his message begins.

> Comfort, comfort my people, says your God.
> Speak tenderly to Jerusalem,
>   and cry to her
> that her warfare is ended,
>   that her iniquity is pardoned,
> that she has received from the Lord's hand
>   double for all her sins.

Here he described a past that had been overcome, and concluded, and forgiven. The guilt had been taken away; the way was thus opened for a liberated future, devoid of past burdens. That was the basis for the comfort for God's people from the mouth of the prophet. Deutero-Isaiah, from all that we know, was a prophet among the exiled Jews in Babylon during the forties, in the sixth century B.C. He saw a change of fortunes made possible by the success of the Persian king, Cyrus, and a very difficult situation in the internal affairs of Babylon. He set forth a better future for the exiled Babylonian Jews who had suffered under foreign power for many decades. He understood that exile as a time in which God had given the people the opportunity to be pardoned for their iniquity which had brought about the fall of Judah and the city of Jerusalem in 587–76 B.C. The past was viewed as "iniquity," and the "warfare" referred to its troubles, which soon would be "ended." Israel's fate had been a hard one, and she had suffered "double" for her sins. Now the iniquities had been compensated for—doubly so. The door of the future was opened, and the Prophet reported that he heard a voice speaking of a way that had been prepared for the people to return home—led by God himself:

> A voice cries:
> "In the wilderness prepare the way of the Lord,
> make straight in the desert a highway for our God."

That has to do with the future. God will establish a straight way, upon which he will lead his people. The remembrance of the Exodus, back in the days of Moses, vibrated within and became a new promise of a renewed existence in the land of promise. This expectation was clothed in the shape of tradition that at the same time became a guarantee, because God had proven himself to be true to his promises.

Certainly this has very little to do with the portrayal of history in the strict sense of the word, but rather with the presuppositions of all historical experience. In Deutero Isaiah, one can begin to sketch the contours of an abstract conception of the extensive relationships between time and subject matter that make possible the perspective of the great summarizing redactions of the historical books in the Old Testament. One realizes that the great historical work that extends from Joshua to II Kings was brought together in Palestine and edited at about the same time, and that the question of the iniquity of the past was greatly stressed in it. One must bear in mind that the Pentateuch came into being a short time later, and looking back to the law given on the mountain of God, the foundations for the postexilic community were laid. By reflecting on the oldest traditions, and in the actual process of gathering these and dealing with them anew, the past was overcome. This process had as its goal the forming of a new future.

The continuum made up of tradition—recognition of iniquity, the experience of divine forgiveness, and the expectation of the future—made it possible for the people of Israel mentally and physically to overcome the severe catastrophe of the Babylonian exile. Moreover, it enabled the Jews to see anew that their whole history was a history with their God, in spite of all their errors and troubles. This historical recognition was woven indissolubly together with the theological points of view. Existence was created in the past by this theological understanding of the way in which the people had gone, and now it had been newly opened again and preserved for them. Deutero-Isaiah can say (48:20),

> Go forth from Babylon, flee from Chaldea,
>   declare this with a shout of joy, proclaim it,
> send it forth to the end of the earth;
>   say, "The Lord has redeemed his servant Jacob!"

In these few verses, an affirming connection is made with unusual conciseness between the historical experience of being set free, or delivered, and a universal theological message addressed to the whole world—a message that Israel should not keep to itself. The world shall see what God will do with his people who had been so nearly humiliated and destroyed. He had set them free from their fate and now once again they are active in the world and must be accepted. One might call that preaching. However, it contains an extension of the horizon of experience which one seeks in vain elsewhere in the Old Testament. Israel's historical experience—being led out of its own land and confronted with the greater world—strengthened its belief that God was a being above all nations. Consequently, the people saw him as the God of the world;

time and history were in his hand. It was not far from that point
to praise of the Creator of space and time, as found in
Deutero-Isaiah (45:11-12):

> Thus says the Lord,
>   the Holy One of Israel, and his Maker:
> "Will you question me about my children,
>   or command me concerning the work of my hands?
> I made the earth,
>   and created man upon it;
> it was my hands that stretched out the heavens,
>   and I commanded all their host."

As a consequence, the Creator of the world became also the
Lord of all order in time and space, and he was the only one who
could give authentic information concerning the future. In this
way they grasped the most ancient matters, whose effects
extend to the end of the world, in terms of the temporal and
spatial. In Deutero-Isaiah, we find those very formulas that are
used to describe God's eternal existence in all contemporary
forms of philosophy. And yet these should not be read and
understood as expressions of eternal, unchangeable power or as
experiences of eternal being, in the sense of some fixed
statistic. For the eternal and ancient is the One who is at work
from the beginning, and he is active in all his deeds and plans,
to the very end. Humanity is not delivered over to him in some
fatalistic resignation—this God speaks, and what he desires, he
makes known. His words are not mythical formulas, but living
expressions of an eternal, yet variable God, who is always at
work in creating that which is new. Deutero-Isaiah gives
expression to that thought (46:9-11):

> Remember the former things of old;
> for I am God, and there is no other;
>   I am God, and there is none like me,
> declaring the end from the beginning
>   and from ancient times things not yet done,

saying, "My counsel shall stand,
   and I will accomplish all my purpose,"
calling a bird of prey from the east,
   the man of my counsel from a far country.
I have spoken, and I will bring it to pass;
   I have purposed, and I will do it.

The last words about the ravenous bird and the man who will serve this God appear to disturb the high flight of the philosophical supertemporal hymn of the beginning. In truth, however, they are the goals of the discourse. God does not remain some abstract intangible entity; he does not hide himself behind the clouds of a loose speculative thought, as the God of philosophy, but announces his activity in a concrete, inexorable, well-planned way, with complete irrevocable certainty. For, indeed, the man from the East was the Persian king, Cyrus, who stormed across the ancient world placing nations under his dominion and creating new orders. However, when the prophet spoke his words, things had not progressed that far; therefore his words were not the cheap echo of some glory-seeking theologian who belatedly declares the signs of the times, but rest upon the certainty of prophetic insight. This certainty has at its basis the unique God of the world who knows how to make use of his tools, either for destruction or for the continuing regulation and transformation of the world.

This is neither historical presentation or hermeneutic of history, in the usual sense of the word—it is concentrated prophecy. In Deutero-Isaiah, we see historical experience woven together with the certainty of a turn in world history. It did not happen by chance. The one who carried it out was the Persian, Cyrus, who was already at work and cloaked in the highest divine authorization (according to Deutero-Isaiah). God had grasped this Cyrus by his right hand. He became the "man of [God's] counsel" and went out to overwhelm the nations (Isa. 45:1). This is not the often-criticized theological glossing-over of political events and leaders. Finally, the prophet speaks not just of his own people, but also of political opponents. It is not a mixture of tactical calculation with mental arrogance that occasions his word, but a prophetic certainty stemming from the affirming God. This prophetic speech is not determined by some religious directive involving heated-up political ideology, with all its wishes and desires, but by his contact with the experienced, empirically apprehended, but not yet regulated power of historical movement. In the prophetic view, this movement is cloaked in the divine experience, although it stands at some distance from historical political calculation. The reality of history is experienced here in its final truth, even if it is difficult to reach that conclusion from rational reconstruction.

The book of Deutero-Isaiah, both in its historical concreteness and its symbolism of detail, presents the ultimate expression of abstract principles within Old Testament prophecy. Normally speaking, its maximum value is not sought in this impulse to abstraction; rather, its real experiences compel one to stand firm. Therefore there are variables in the conflict with historical reality; yet there are always appropriate means of expression at hand.

To be sure, Cyrus did bring down the Babylonian kingdom (539 B.C.), after which he also granted extensive rights to the exiled Jews in Babylon. As far as we know, he allowed the rebuilding of the temple in Jerusalem and probably also the return of Jewish families— as many as wanted to go. However, twenty years after the fall of Babylon (520 B.C.), the temple still lay in ruins, and there could be no talk of rebuilding the wall of the city or renewing community life. This was the time of the prophets Haggai and Zechariah.

There is a series of eight so-called night visions of the prophet Zechariah (Zech. 1:7–6:8). For the first time, an impressionable symbolical means of expression is created that would later be developed fully in apocalyptic literature. We must keep in focus, though, that the beginning of this thoroughly historically related form of expression was not directed to the distant future, but had as its goal an expectation of an immediate imminent future, which was then joined with an impressionistic description of the present. Two of the visions—the first and the eighth—which serve as a framework around the other six, speak of horses and chariots that roam across the land. It is not difficult to recognize that we have here the mold for those apocalyptic riders, which in the New Testament apocalypse, the Revelation of John (6:1-8), are the means for carrying out the last acts of history as they bring destruction and misfortune. Their prototypes in Zechariah are commissioned of God primarily to observe the world and to inform him concerning all the activities taking place. Secondly, they are to execute a judgment of the people. It would take us too far afield here to analyze the visions of Zechariah, which elucidate the internal political power relationships in Jerusalem in February 519, through such symbolical presentations as a measuring rod, oil lamps, and flying objects, a scroll, and even a woman in a jug, who symbolizes evil. The prophecy of Zechariah stands in a transition stage between Deutero-Isaiah and the later apocalyptic.

Deutero-Isaiah now viewed the God of Israel, who once had been limited just to Israel as a nation, as the one who rules over all of space and time, and proclaimed him to be the God of the world. As the Creator of the world, he alone would determine history. Zechariah, in Jerusalem, also believed that the world powers were ruled by God, but his experience had changed somewhat. He was moved not only by hope in the liberating act of Cyrus, the world conqueror, but also by fear of inner political divisions. He realized that the world powers once again could become a threat to Israel and little Jerusalem and its way of life. The leading personalities of Jerusalem were not faultless—the inhabitants were fighting for their very existence, and the temple still had not been rebuilt. The basic attitude that would shape Jerusalem-Judean Judaism from now on in the postexilic period, during the rule of the Persians and later under the Greeks and the Romans, was established in this way. Israel was a nation thrown into the whirlpool of the historical movements of the world—dependent and limited in its response and existing under various conditions and potentates. It saw its innermost nature—its relationship to God—threatened again and again and also faced the danger of being delivered over to one or another global power of the day. From the time of Alexander the Great, the little state of Israel had been caught up into the orbit of the major powers and left politically lame. The danger of a great conqueror had become a potential threat that was partially realized under Diodotus, in the third century B.C., but more massively under Antiochus IV, Epiphanes (175–164 B.C.), who occupied Jerusalem and sought to hellenize its cult.

e. New Dimensions: The Apocalyptic

In the second century B.C., the last writing in the Old Testament, the Book of Daniel was completed. The first six chapters are a series of tendentious narratives in which the wise Daniel and his friends at the Babylonian court play an important role. Following chapter 6, there is an entirely different section, making use of the language and imagery of the apocalyptic. Behind this independent, but not arbitrary, way of presentation, filled with images and symbols, there stands the conflict of real problems in the history of the world politics of the time. Chapter 7, especially, influenced schools and inspired the writing of apocalyptic manuscripts in many ways. For Israel, a little nation, it provided a way to settle accounts with the world powers whose inroads had been empirically experienced since the end of Jewish independence with the conquest by the Babylonians in 587-76 B.C. From the sea, which elsewhere in the ancient Orient and in the Old Testament symbolized chaos and the mass of enemy peoples, there arose four terrible beasts, which symbolized the Babylonian, Median, Persian, and Greek empires. We cannot discuss here the prior history of these symbols, which stand for the four kingdoms, which are closely related to the concept of four world periods, characterized in turn by four metals. (They are the constitutive elements of a statue representing the world kingdoms, in Daniel 2). Only a few instructive remarks can be given here.

The idea of four world ages is also known in the Greek realm. Hesiod's *Works and Days* (106–200), sets forth four races, which constitute all the ages of the world and are characterized by four metals: gold, silver, brass (bronze), and iron. This same theory of four periods of metal appears later in Iranian literature. The Book of Daniel, however, does not have in mind world ages in the sense of some undetermined historical dimension, but world kingdoms as historicopolitical entities. There is even a firmly established model for the concept of the four kingdoms. The four-kingdom scheme of Assyria, Media, Persia, and Macedonia also was known in Roman literature, such as the Punic history of Appian (Pun. c. 132). Therefore, it represents a collection of the leading superpowers of the ancient Orient, dating back at the latest to the ninth century B.C., and includes the kingdom of Alexander, which had been conquered by the Persians. To be sure, the Medians do not play an equal role, and the Babylonians are missing altogether. The fact that in Daniel, the Assyrians are replaced by the Babylonians, can be attributed to the role Babylon played with the Jews in the sixth century. It appears quite probable that this pattern of four kingdoms was of oriental origin and was not original in the Old Testament. Daniel made use of it in setting forth his apocalyptic conceptual world and also adopted current theories concerning the course of the periods of human and world history. Giving names of metal to the different ages originated not in Israel or Greece, but in the Iranian-Indian realm.

The Book of Daniel elaborated upon this borrowed material with its own unique style and added new elements to it. Hence the picture of four world kingdoms, represented by four animals, was accomplished under the influence of ancient oriental skills of presentation. However, Daniel presents a sequence of pictures, which captured the course of world history and represent it as increasingly cruel and horrible. If one thinks that this downhill view probably was not evident in sources outside Israel, then let him turn to Hesiod's emphasis on a decline that led from gold to iron. By adopting the scheme of the four kingdoms, it is quite certain that the Book of Daniel also held the idea of a declining tendency, demonstrating a very pessimistic view of the course of world history, which should not be viewed as cyclical in nature, but as uniquely linear.

In Daniel 7, there is no doubt that the horrible fourth beast with the horns was an allusion to the worldwide kingdom of the Greeks under Alexander and his successors. In the horns, one of which had been broken off and replaced (Dan. 7:8), we see reflected the complicated and jealous history of the Diadochi. The last horn is portrayed with human eyes and a mouth that spoke great things. Other texts of Daniel help us to see that hidden here is Antiochus IV, a contemporary of the apocalyptic writer. Then the scene changes. Following the description of the powerful and mighty of the earth as animals, we see a scene in heaven. God himself, the Ancient of Days, sits in the middle of his heavenly court and holds a judgment, a prototype of that described in the Revelation of John, chapter 1. The world kingdoms lose their power; the beast with the horns is put to death and burned. The seer then beholds one in the likeness of a man, who is carried upon the clouds of heaven and is brought before the Ancient of Days. He is granted power for all time and embodies a "kingdom of the saints of the Most High"—a holy people who would emerge to dedicate themselves to the service of their God and who would supersede the world powers that had been shown in animal form.

Therefore, that is the great hope—the expectation of the Jewish people, which had been expressed passionately in apocalyptic forms since the oppression of Antiochus IV. There would be an end of the powers on earth, a judgment of God, and then an eternal kingdom of peace, represented with human characteristics and symbolized by one like unto a man, to whom God grants all powers. It is evident that this "one like unto a man" in Daniel 7:13 is only a symbol in contrast to the animals that represented the kingdoms; in later apocalyptic writings he takes on a distinct personality, as "the Son of man." (This is especially true in the Ethiopian Book of Enoch). The Son of man then was brought into close relationship with the messianic king from the tribe of David whom Israel had long expected. Thus the "kingdom of the saints of the Most High" in Daniel is our first encounter with the idea of a "messianic kingdom" that would follow the end of world history—a rule of the Messiah, in which only the chosen of God and the most dedicated would participate.

It should be noted that the sequence of the eschatological final acts in the drama of the end-time was differentiated still further within the framework of Jewish apocalyptic. There emerged the idea of a limited thousand-year messianic kingdom of peace, or a perfected condition of the world before the end of the age should come—the resurrection, the last judgment, and the New Creation. In this way, the thousand-year, or messianic, kingdom became a transition stage in which all earthly existence would be transformed into perfection, all the expectations of the righteous would be fulfilled, and Satan would be bound. On the basis of Revelation 20:4-6, this part of the expectation concerning the end of time found its way into Christian thought and enriched it with various shades of meaning concerning the idea of a consummation of the world, be it in the limited sense of "a thousand years" (Chiliasm) or in the secular sense of faith in the goal of uninterrupted progress.

Essential elements of the different kinds of apocalyptic expectations of Judaism also made their way into Paul's view of the end of the world in I Corinthians 15:20-28. There also, the goal is the replacement of earthly powers by a form of rule directed by God, which will place the seal of God's victory upon the world. God will found a kingdom that will have more spiritual than physical characteristics, and in contrast to the messianic kingdom, it will be less tangible. Whether any one of these conceptions of apocalyptic can be compared directly with the "kingdom of God," the "rule of God," or the "heavenly kingdom of God" that Jesus taught, involves a special problem, which in turn requires a particular explanation.

When we look back, it is easy to see that the apocalyptic expectation of the end in the Old Testament is much more than wild speculation. At its beginning stands a historical experience, which in Deutero-Isaiah was expanded into a view of God as One who encompasses all peoples; who from the very beginning ruled over time and space; who proclaimed his plans; who saw his people and the people of the world as linked together. A few decades later, that which was formulated here as hopeful expectation took on the character of a gloomy prognosis in Zechariah, because the historical experience in and around Israel did not allow the prophets to view an unbroken line of God's will for deliverance as being possible. The intensification of the Persian and Greek-Hellenistic world politics caused the little state of Israel, centered around Jerusalem, to become a political football among the superpowers both at home and abroad. Now at last, world politics took on a negative light and was portrayed as a very bruising battle for power that could be brought to an end only by God himself. The hope of such an intervention was linked with the expectation that the truly faithful ones of God would survive and become the nucleus for a new period of humankind that would be taken over by the "saints of the Most High."

The portrayal of history in the Old Testament has been dealt with here rather broadly; only in a few places has it been handled in a more exact paradigmatic sense. Yet we have seen that it corresponds indeterminably to the historical phases of that time and the experiences that Israel encountered. The early period, characterized by the lengendary stories about the great personalities and the tribes and the people in their beginning days, was replaced by the early monarchical period, with its psychologically more exact ways of presentation. (Tactical calculations were not overlooked.) This was especially true of kings Saul, David, and Solomon. The prophets' experience of history, which arose in Israel's conflict with its surrounding world and with the world powers that threatened it, sparked a comparison with what Israel had been, what Israel should expect from her God based on tradition and heritage, what he had promised, and what now stood before her. The inevitable catastrophe of the Babylonian exile—the total loss of political independence—signified a turning point that appeared to destroy all expectations. Yet God would conquer even this, because Israel had discovered, in the experience of sin and forgiveness, that Yahweh had shown himself to be constant, and the Lord and Creator of the world, who promised a New Creation after the days of catastrophe. He would do the expected thing before the people of the world and completely rehabilitate his people. That the universal politics of the world powers of late antiquity nearly had brought the Jewish people to the edge of extinction did not mean the end of Israel's existential theological thought at all. On the contrary, she now raised her expectations even higher, to the certainty of God's immediate intervention, which would culminate in his eternal rule.

f. The New Testament

It is not difficult, in this treatment of the historical understanding of the Old Testament in all its various stages, enriched by the thought-forms of apocalyptic and late Jewish literature, to draw certain observations for the understanding of history and its form of presentation in the New Testament. A direct comparison with the Old Testament is not as easy, for there is no direct point of connection between the two, and thus they cannot be viewed in a literary-historical continuum. For the literary witnesses collected in the New Testament are to be distinguished from those of the Old Testament—their origins, conceptions, and forms are very different, for they have their roots in other periods and other epochs. The events described in the Old Testament took place in a period of about 1000 years, from 1100 to 100 B.C. In contrast, the writing of the New Testament, which grew out of the coming of Jesus Christ and gave a direct witness to his appearance and work, took place over a period of 100 years, generally estimated as being from A.D. 30 to 130. In the Old Testament, we see sources and witnesses of a long history of a people; in the New Testament, we encounter reports, transmissions, letters, and transactions that have their base in the experience of a course of events with a very different time span. This series of events had their beginning in the work of Jesus and ended with the growing consolidations of the first Christian churches.

When one ponders this, it still is very surprising that there are so many different *Gattungen*, speech forms, and literary formations in the New Testament. Very few direct comparisons can be made with similar literary *Gattungen* of classical antiquity. Therefore in the New Testament, to a great extent, we have a *sui generis* literature, although there certainly are cases where the history-of-traditions process is fully related to the conditions of tradition in the Old Testament.

The tradition of the Gospels is made up of small units, most of a narrative type, but frequently detached or interspersed with discourse sections. The oldest of these Gospels, the one "According to Mark," demonstrates that these small units are relatively independent but that, in a limited sense, they

already have a firm "canonical" sequence. At the beginning
stands the baptism and the temptation of Jesus and his first
work in Galilee. In the middle of the Gospel is found the
transfiguration story. Soon thereafter follows the movement to
Jerusalem and Jesus' work there, and on to the passion, death,
and resurrection. Should one see the work of an editor in the
associations made within the tradition, one cannot consequently reject a "biographical" sketch of the life of Jesus, which
had first, Galilee, and finally, Jerusalem and Judea as its major
emphasis. The Gospels of Matthew and Luke base their
presentation on the order given in Mark, but elaborate upon
this to some extent with their own discourse sections, which
may have belonged at some time to an independent tradition
(so-called "discourse source"). To this source are attributed the
Sermon on the Mount (Matthew) and the so-called Sermon on
the Plain (Luke). There are also numerous narrative passages
not found in Mark, such as those concerning the birth of Jesus
and his early life (Matt. 1:2; Luke 1:2), and his activity in Galilee
(the so-called Lukan travel narrative, Luke 9:51–18:14). One
should also note the numerous, yet different resurrection
accounts (Matt. 28:11-20; Luke 24:13-53).

We need also address ourselves to Acts, as the
continuation of the Gospel of Luke, which has as its purpose to
set forth the history of the mission of Peter (Acts 2–12) and Paul
(Acts 13–28), starting with the ascension of Jesus, the first
Jerusalem church (Acts 1), and the coming of the Holy Spirit
(Acts 2). In many cases speeches created by Luke are placed in
the mouths of the leading figures.

John stands apart from these writings just mentioned.
Without a doubt, it is the youngest of the Gospels and takes
over just a few narratives from the others, and even these are
changed in part. Most striking in John's Gospel is his style of
composition, which involves a more extensive, reflective
pattern of thought concerning the words of Jesus, but above all,

concerning Jesus' person, his purpose and validity for Israel, Judaism, and the world. There are long dialogues attached to short narratives, which have as their goal to place the person of Jesus in the light of a special problem situation, a particular direction of faith, or a controversy. This is particularly evident in John 3, in the discourse that Jesus had with the Pharisee Nicodemus concerning "being born anew" (John 3:1-21). We would also make mention of John the Baptist's discourse to the disciples (John 3:22-36). The problem concerning the "Samaritan community," which had separated itself from Jerusalem and had its holy place on Mount Gerizim, is dealt with by Jesus in his discourse with the Samaritan woman (John 4). Problems concerning the Jewish community were determined by the discourse concerning the healing of the sick man at the Pool of Bethesda (John 5). It is very possible that the long discourse about the bread of life at the conclusion of the feeding of the five thousand (John 6) is addressed to problems concerning the sacramental understanding of the Lord's Supper. Jesus appears as the Light of the World (John 8) and as the Good Shepherd (John 10). The redaction of a many-faceted tradition and the encounter with the work and person of Jesus, in the view of the Evangelist John, reached its final high point in the so-called farewell discourses of Jesus (John 14–16), as well as in the high priestly prayer of Jesus (John 17), which is placed just before the beginning of his passion. This prayer also serves the purpose of determining the place of Jesus in reference to his Father, in the course of Johannine theology. The Gospel concludes with an independent passion narrative and a unique resurrection appearance.

The purpose of this brief overview of the Gospel literature of the New Testament was to submit the various basic presentations of the appearance of Jesus in the four Gospels, as based on well-known and shaped traditions. Their composition—especially the redactional work of the Gospels can be readily compared with the redaction of the tradition in the Old

Testament writings. Today, the intention of this redaction has been made the object of research, but there is no solidarity of opinion concerning the normative principles that the Evangelists may have been following in their work of compilation. A rough reassessment would allow us to say that Mark was writing against the background of the Jerusalem primitive community; Matthew, from a principally Jewish-Christian milieu; Luke had in mind a basically Gentile audience, which was not limited to the Palestinian realm. John, in contrast, was writing for churches in Syria and Asia Minor.

One who reads and compares the translations of the Gospels can soon make a judgment as to which passages give one a sense of the historical Jesus. Numerous scenes and words in Mark, as well as in Matthew and Luke, testify to the unusual effects of the personality of Jesus in various situations. They do not report some excessively contrived presentation of a miracle worker with a supernatural glow. Rather, we confront a man whose winsome ways attracted some people and caused enigmatic misunderstandings and disenchancement among others, including his own disciples. It is quite unlikely that this picture of Jesus is the work of a later generation, who neither saw him nor heard him. This is true even though I have a high regard for the literary sensitivity of early Christian authors.

The case is quite different with John, whose style included taking over small narrative units such as those found in the Synoptics, but then following his own high-flying thoughts. He placed words in the mouth of Jesus which we would term as having a literary purpose. Here we encounter a style used extensively among ancient authors—one in which discourses were used to create controversial problems. The authority of the one speaking would bring greater weight or validity to the problem situation involved. The Johannine discourses of Jesus therefore are consciously formed in accordance with one direction of early Christian theology. This direction can be summarized briefly in the statement that the proclaimer became that which was proclaimed, or that the one speaking became the object of thought and faith. In this way there came into being the authoritative "I am" sayings, which put all that was proclaimed on an equal footing with the person of the Proclaimer: I am the way, the truth, and the life; I am the bread of life, the light of the world, the true vine; and finally, I and the Father are one.

The controversy of the most recent New Testament research has its real starting point in the debate concerning which should receive the higher value—this "Christ of faith," as he appears in the reflective theology of the early Christian thinkers and writers, or the "historical Jesus," whose words are much more difficult to understand as well as to determine with certainty. If one goes so far as to assume that the "historical Jesus" of the Synoptic Gospels—Mark, Matthew, and Luke—is the product of early Christian church tradition, then the personality of Jesus disappears completely from the realm of scholarly research. We then must conclude that in all the Gospels, we confront only the Jesus of the church's tradition and no longer have any picture of the man from Nazareth.

One marvels how New Testament research has been blinded for such a long time as the result of conclusions made concerning the circumstances surrounding the origins of the Gospels and the conscious effort to give a late date to the formation of their factual content. Relatively simple reflection would help one see that the unusual spiritual power that grasped the early Christians after the death of Jesus was not just the fruit of intensive mental processes on their part, but must have been the perceptible effect of an undeniable experience with the "person" of Jesus. This should be a warning to research, in terms of being blinded to the import of the "historical Jesus" as the normative influence. However, it should be added here that those researchers who have this blind spot cannot be certified as primarily pursuing a historical interest. They are much more motivated by the conviction that the person and work of Jesus ought not to be primarily understood from the standpoint of his encountering, shaping, or transforming the Jewish tradition. The real impulse of Christian theology should be sought at the point where faith in Jesus Christ came into conflict with the surrounding world— where it proved to be the message (kerygma) of a New Man. Thus it happened that the complicated line of thought of the New Testament letters, especially those of Paul, had as lasting an impact on the understanding of the work and person of Jesus as did the words that are characterized in the Gospels as being those of Jesus himself. The old debate concerning "Jesus and Paul," or sharpened to "Jesus or Paul," will never find an answer as long as one is not ready to start with the assumption that the development of the message of the historical Jesus is the valid object of New Testament faith and research, and to view its distinctiveness and complexity as being significant. There should be no possibilty of pushing the historical Jesus aside in favor of a "kerygmatic theology."

All these questions are involved directly in the basic question concerning the methodology of New Testament research. The question is whether this research should be guided by a horizon of thought and faith that has been determined by theology or by philosophy—not to mention dogmatics. One could ask whether hermeneutical premises should determine the declarations of research beyond which one cannot, without hermeneutically colored glasses, attempt to advance in seeking to comprehend the words of Jesus against the background of the Jewish, and to a certain extent, the hellenistic-oriented traditions of his time. Of course, within that realm is a readiness to declare the tradition of the New Testament reliable as to Jesus' person and work. That does not rule out the consideration of a process of redaction that might have been carried out on the tradition. Certainly it would be impossible ever to rediscover the actual words of Jesus written down in official form. However, that does not rule out the fact

that the intentionality of his discourse can be grasped, in
contrast to other lines of tradition and thought patterns of his
time.

In this sense, the establishing of the contemporary
historical authenticity of the New Testament tradition,
especially the Gospels, and including Acts (we cannot speak
here in the full sense of the Epistles), is of major importance.
This is especially true if our major concern is to question the
New Testament concerning its relationship to time and history.
For the answer cannot be separated from the presuppositions
that determined time then, and those addressed by Jesus and
the New Testament witnesses. The attempt, fully legitimate
from a historical standpoint, must be made to include Jesus in
the intellectual movements of his day and to observe how he,
himself, encountered the demands of his environment, the
history of his people, and the Roman world power. Only then
can the unusual nature of his total personality, which left such a
deep impression among his contemporaries, emerge. We may
only suggest here that the current view—that Jesus lived in
expectation of the end and that his message was basically
eschatological—is a bit too simple and that essential components of his work do not fit into that kind of analysis. The mere
fact that it is not possible to place Jesus in any of the major
groups of his day—apocalypticists, Pharisees, disciples of John,
or the Essenes—should make it clear that the tradition
concerning him is accurate. He placed himself outside the
realm of all these groups and, as the New Testament tradition
shows, pronounced a judgment on each of them and attributed
to them, at best, only partial truth.

Jesus penetrated more deeply into the conflicts of the
intellectual and political parties of his time than he would or
could, had he been just any fellow combatant following a
particular party line. That is attested to by the Gospels in all
desired clarity. Jesus argued with special interest groups and
parties; yet the tradition attributes to him a certain indepen-

dence over against the supporters of these groups—those who
sought to elicit from him a messianic confession (Mark 12:35-37)
or those who sought to involve him in the sophistry of the
Sadducees (Mark 12:18-27) or those who, indeed, sought to
bring him into conflict with the Roman state (Mark 12:13-17).
This was usually done by a deliberate rhetorical device. One
misunderstands if one attributes such controversies to the
apologetic interests of the primitive church alone and views
them as being very unlikely in reference to Jesus himself. How
else would Jesus have drawn a line between himself and his
surroundings, if not by just such wise outmaneuvering of his
opponents or those who debated with him? Generally, the
Gospels make it clear that Jesus was not prepared to give in to
any of the expected or, perhaps from the point of view of his
followers, desired religious or political revolutionary plans that
were constantly being formulated and also being rooted out.
And yet he desired to bring about a transformation, and he was
convinced that the time was ripe for a fundamental reorientation. But this would not occur by means of politics, or through
society, or through force. Jesus reached back into the tradition
of Israel, placing a great emphasis on the Old Testament and
the expectation of "repentance" and "conversion," and
inscribed upon the shield of the conscience the commands to
love God and neighbor. He saw those commands as the key for
the fulfillment of Old Testament expectations. As much as Jesus
himself may have related such deliberations to his own people
Israel and their reorientation on the basis of their own
developed tradition, they still bear within themselves the
tendency of a universal human significance. Precisely in the
absence of a revolutionary apocalyptic—a politically radicalized
expectation—ground was laid for a universal human dimension
for man's experience of God and redemption. To take this
comparison further: The universal God of Deutero-Isaiah was
experienced anew, and the return of Israel to this God renewed

and prepared the way, in a spiritual sense, for the prophecy that Deutero-Isaiah had already spoken: God has redeemed his servant, Jacob.

This prophetic intention of Jesus, which can be read from the Gospel accounts, hardly can be viewed as the product of the early church's interpretation. For that would mean entrusting the work of Jesus to the anonymous process of thought within the unestablished young Christian churches. It is much more believable to attribute this prophetic impulse to the discourse of an extraordinarily overwhelming personality. His contemporaries are able to follow him only with hesitation and at times, only with inadequate mental presuppositions. The well-known first sentence from Rudolf Bultmann's *Theology of the New Testament* reads, "The proclamation of Jesus belongs to the presuppositions of New Testament theology and is not, itself, a part of it." The reverse of this sentence, based on historical reflection, would have far greater weight: "The proclamation of Jesus is the foundation of New Testament theology and underlies all its various means of expression." Bultmann takes into consideration the difficulty of his theological position a few sentences later, when he speaks of "the kerygma of the primitive community" and concedes the historical point: "To these historical presuppositions belong, of course, the appearance and the proclamation of Jesus, and in this sense the proclamation of Jesus must be included in the presentation of New Testament theology."

Here at last the conflict that exists in the relationship between theological and historical presentation of New Testament factual material is made clear. Thus it seems that thorough study of that relationship is justified here. For we must dismiss immediately the suspicion that Christian faith can be loosed from historical presuppositions or that it should be seen as a secondary formation of the theology of the church, based on a historical occurrence—the appearance of Jesus. Some hold this to be true even though they would not view the form created by the church as the most decisive form of this faith. We obtain a close-up view of that kind of suspicion in the third sentence of Bultmann's theology: "For New Testament theology consists in the unfolding of those ideas by means of which Christian faith makes sure of its own object, basis, and consequences. But Christian faith did not exist until there was a Christian kerygma; i.e., a kerygma proclaiming Jesus Christ as God's eschatological salvific act—specifically Jesus Christ the Crucified and Risen One."

At first glance, it may appear that the significance of Jesus' death and resurrection was first recognized and defined in all fullness after those events had taken place. All the pertinent predictions of suffering given by Jesus in the Gospels have been written off by critical scholarship as later additions. This forces us back to the difficult question: Which presuppositions could have made possible this interpretation of the death and resurrection of Jesus? Which one would have brought into being the Christian kerygma and faith as Bultmann views it? For the shameful death on the cross and the all too quick appearance of resurrection stories would have aroused suspicion and would not have lent themselves to the grounding of faith, but would have pushed it into the twilight zone. The danger existed as confirmed by Paul in I Corinthians 1:18, that all this might have been called "foolishness." That death and resurrection were understood as "salvation acts" cannot be deduced from the death and resurrection of just any man. In a greater way, those who had experienced Jesus—those who had heard him and were in his confidence—saw in the events of his death and resurrection the most unusual confirmation of the fact that this Jesus could lay claim to the validity that already was present in his message. The death and resurrection did not create the kerygma, but fulfilled it.

By necessity, the New Testament theology begins where the ground is laid for a kerygma—in Jesus' own message. Consequently, Christian faith also begins there—where the word of this Jesus, who appeared in Palestine as a historical personality, encounters a faith response. If one should attempt to "pull the rug from under" this "historical Jesus" by terming the Gospels a product of the primitive church and thereby consigning the historical Jesus to the darkness of historical uncomprehension, one makes the error of confusing the redaction of the tradition concerning the historical Jesus with the history and historicity of Jesus himself.

Here we arrive at the most serious point of the hermeneutical discussion: What is history; what is the faith that furnishes the foundation for history? Is history the factual event, or is it that which we experience about that event, in the necessary fragmentation of the history of tradition? Only the last appears to give us full assurance and is the very thing that lies before us in express form. On what do we found our faith? Do we found it only on the testimony of the developed tradition, or on the basic event behind this tradition in its pure factual nature? Here there seems to be no alternative. As we have indicated, it should be understood that the apparently insoluble relationship between the historical event and its transmission would be cause for earnest doubt, if the event and tradition were brought into a controllable incongruity. The three Synoptic Gospels contain a fullness of individual material, and all set forth pictures of Jesus that are very similar in nature, and complementary. There are variations within the tradition, but no differences in purpose. The hermeneutical purpose of the individual Evangelist is controllable, but such controls do not produce a disharmony that is contrary to historical credibility. More cannot be expected of a tradition that has found its form in reference to the custom of ancient transmission of tradition. These small units, shaped in the oral period, continue on in a polished form and are collected and joined into a unity. Redactional work is not excluded in this process, but it did not play a determining role. On the contrary, the question of the oldest foundation stone in the ancient

times. This evidence, although not overwhelming, still affords the searching thinker room for action in interpretation, which can be limited through the judgments of contemporaries or through the direct effects of successive events and developments. In spite of this, as already earlier set forth, the task of the historian is the determination of the relationship between cause and effect, especially those effects that are direct parts of an event—intended, to be sure, but in no way penetrating its full extent, and least of all, controlling it. The presentation of a stratum of events will take place by necessity as the investigative or descriptive understanding of the historical thinker sees it as being correct, or at least worthy of consideration. Finally, he will place the emphasis on his own power of conviction and seek to acquire meaning for the described connection of events; he is concerned with bestowing validity upon the event. He first seeks to place that which is described in a more extensive connection. However, that necessarily pushes the event out of the area of limited empirical data and its casual relationship, into the dimension of a higher or more comprehensive value, which still must be related causally or directly to a definite event. If once a stratum of a sufficiently understandable and clear plausibility is found, then empirical data can be inserted into this stratum only with a degree of relative probability. Then the historian, going beyond his historiographical duty, desires to give the reflective observer enough room to understand the described event. In this process the historian goes beyond hermeneutic to become a "philosopher," in that he evaluates data, and at the same time makes use of comprehensive and general logic—a process that can be analyzed at each step of the way.

This process, which at its deepest is rooted in the uniqueness of human thought patterns, was described by Friedrich Schiller in his famous inaugural lecture at Jena in 1789, "What Is Universal History and Why Study It?"

As often therefore and with what pleasant success he (the philosophical thinker) renews his attempt to link the past with the present, the more he becomes inclined to connect what he sees as the relationship of cause and effect to means and purpose. One appearance after another helps one begin to escape the danger of blind weakness—freedom without law and to place oneself as a proper link in an harmonious whole (which of course is only present in the imagination). Soon he finds it difficult to persuade himself that this succession of appearances which takes on such regularity and purpose in his imagination, in reality may deny these qualities. It becomes difficult for him to place again under the blind rule of necessity that which had begun, under the borrowed light of understanding, to acquire such a clear form. Therefore he takes this harmony from out of himself and transplants it into the order of things, i.e., he introduces a rational purpose into the course of the world and a teleological principle into world history. With this, he traverses it one time and examines it against every appearance which that great show place offers him. He sees it confirmed through a thousand determining facts and refuted by just as many. But as long as many important connecting links are missing in the series of world changes, just so long will fate hold back final information concerning so many events. He declares the problem as undecided and that attitude prevails which offers to reason the highest satisfaction and to the heart, the greatest bliss [86:222,3].

The dominant thought of this section of Schiller's speech is that it is reason that affects the order of things in the wide field of world history. Seen apart from this, at the very beginning, historians and philosophers place the principle of cause in the critical light. Schiller spoke of intention—of cause and effect— as the means and the purpose, where they are recognized and understood as such. Where that happens, a series of postponements of consideration takes place. For by no means must an appearance that occurs one time, as a cause, necessarily be interpreted as a conscious introduction of a means to an end. An effect that is observed once must never be viewed as the purpose of some action. Here false evaluation can lead to a false judgment of personalities and courses of action. This question is of great significance for the evaluation of the biblical circumstances about which we will speak later.

What Schiller ascribed to the "philosophical spirit" is valid also, as has been shown, for the writer of history, who in a slightly different way becomes the one who interprets his subject. It is also valid, of course, in a special way for the philosophy of history. For most philosophical questions that are brought to bear on history, and to which history must give an answer, are the very kind that Schiller described as alluring to the "philosphical mind." Just prior to the section quoted above, he declared,

> The philosophical mind cannot while away the time for a long period in the material of world history. A new drive is active within him which strives for harmony—which irresistibly excites him. All his own rational nature is assimilated around him and every appearance that comes to him has a great effect, which he recognizes and lifts up into thought.

Actually, one must admit flatly that the best and highest accomplishments of so-called historical writing are frequently those stemming from "philosophy of history." Such accomplishments are achieved by means of comprehensive mental endeavors, which work through the material until a convincing interpretation of the events appears. In this way the contemporary reader is furnished a rational interpretation of that mixture of connected facts, intended order, and intended meaning. In truth, however, to a high degree, that is a hermeneutical process, which makes a strike into the philosophical realm and perfects an apparently unquestioned view of history, thus offering "the highest satisfaction of reason" and "the greatest bliss to the heart." This feeling of bliss can be perceived when one addresses each cardinal question of

humanity that has any connection to philosophical decisions—
questions concerning the meaning of life, of history, of the
future, of progress, of continuity or discontinuity of developments, of law, of accident or freedom of life and its formative
powers, of fate and providence, of the role of personality in
history, of the origin and end of humanity, of the fall of peoples
and cultures, of the meaning of the riddle of time, which seems
incomprehensible and moves forward and backward in
unending lines. What is the goal of history? Is there such a
thing? What is the meaning of suffering in history? What is
justice, and what balances it? Does humanity await judgment,
or is Schiller's poem, "Resignation," correct in saying that
world history is world judgment?

Each of these key words could be expanded into an
independent treatment. Much has been thought and written
about each of these difficult problems of humanity. Here we
cannot take on the task of pursuing the many branches of
human thought—not even the Western philosophy of history,
with all of its thinkers. Just the full list of great names—Augus-
tine, Joachim of Floris, Thomas Aquinas, Luther—would
prevent us from doing more than investigate the differences in
their philosphical origins and consequences, in order to
interpret their meaning for time and history. The actual
development of a philosophical system of thought, which also
included the philosophy of history, brought about the
Enlightenment. After that time, none of those wise men
neglected any problem that concerned history, even though
they all did not make time and history their exclusive theme.
Characteristically, in their chief works, men of the highest
systematic mental accomplishments have demonstrated no
inclination toward that which we call "history." This can be said
of Descartes, Leibniz, and even Kant. Voltaire and Comte
came a bit closer to the problem. In the German realm, Hegel
built a complete system, including a high degree of historical
philosophical apparatus. The great contribution of historical

research in the nineteenth century also influenced the construction of systems of world-views. The foundations of these systems often were not deduced from historically related factors but were assimilated unquestioningly, according to the thinker's own conceptions. This was true of Marx and, in a different way, of his contemporary Nietzsche. In like manner, we exclude those at the beginning of this century—Spengler, Troeltsch, Max Weber—although history was their domain. If one attempts to follow these lines even farther (as far as one may use here the concept of line) one hesitates, for fear that by accidental choice, one would stress one side too heavily. The names of Jaspers, Heidegger, Litt, and Tillich indicate distinctive directions and cannot always be pinpointed in reference to general introductory positions. For them and also for many others, Schiller's *Intellectual Situation of the Time* (his writing of 1931) became the starting point and the object of their historical philosophical contribution. In this list, we do not find the professional theologians such as Troeltsch and Tillich, who were concerned with theology alone. Yet all these thinkers, whether they expressed it or not, were heirs of a system of categories related to time and history, which had been molded by biblical thought and which was tied very closely to Western thought. They dealt, of course, with these categories, analyzed and drew up problems based on them, and yet axiomatically, these were found throughout their work; without them their systems would have been empty. For what they termed "time" and "history" rested upon a recognized stratum of presentation—an apparently indisputable consciousness of history and "view of history" which was actively at work as a valid form of thought in the religious, or more precisely, the Christian sources of tradition. A retreat from these conceptual ideas for purposes of communication and understanding would have been impossible and would have led to chaos.

The most dominant factor of all philosophy of history is "time"—itself an abstraction, although of high empirical value, yet that which Kant concedes as a form of intuition *a priori*. Over against that is the other *a priori* form of intuition—space. Philosophers of history have been aware of it but it has never been of burning interest to them—much to their detriment. Some statements of Schiller once again will illustrate this inner force which impresses the concept of time upon the "philosophical mind." In fact, these sentences are a continuation of the passage cited above.

> Indeed we need no reminder that a final scheme of the history of the world is expected in the last times. A hasty use of this great mass of material by the researcher of history could lead very easily to the temptation to do violence to the events. Thus this happy epoch of world history would be made more distant by a too hasty precipitation. However one cannot take notice too early of this lucid but neglected side of world history. Through it one becomes related to the highest object of all human striving. In quiet consideration of this goal, even if it is just a possibility, the diligence of the researcher is granted lively stimulus and renewal. Even the smallest concern will be important to him as he perceives the way or leads someone who comes later along that way in solving the problem of world order and in confronting the highest spirit in its most beautiful effect.

That which is expressed here in emphatic speech is inspired by the deepest conviction that world history is moving toward a goal. This goal will be comprehended by thinkers and witnesses who are able to perceive the course of world history in its greatest dimensions. If this great critrion which only later generations could possess were to be used recklessly, then one could be led very quickly into error—one could "do violence to the events" or attempt to accelerate world history in consideration of a goal based on one's own estimates. That this concept of acceleration is a concern of the most recent historical research might be noted here. We see it in the characteristic way one time period quickly changes into another. In modern times, changes in the course of history follow one another even more quickly. There is an apparent or actual "acceleration" of the courses of inner history, which in earlier periods moved much more slowly. We must touch here also on the question as to whether one must deduce the fullness of the chain of events so hastily arrived at, and grounded and shaded in meaning in other ways from modern treatments, such as those which "accelerate" history, or even more from the determining power of history itself. For the technical conquering of the world has led not only to an acceleration of the flow of time through quicker means of communication, but it has contributed also to a shrinking of the consciousness of space, in which the possibility of conquering great distances in short periods of time plays an essential part. That must result in reverberations on the historical process and its interconnected state of influence.

But what Schiller called acceleration was not related to this effective short-lived nature of world historical impressions and decisions; it was directed at the attempt of the philosophically schooled historian to judge hastily and to determine, in an anticipatory way, the goal of world history from his own point of view. Not only should he keep this real but unreachable goal clearly before him, but he should feel that he is a fellow worker along with others who, through their work and evaluation, help to prepare for and to perfect the final decision.

With such words, of course, Schiller stands in fundamental contrast to later and more modern historians, who desire to get along without such a conception of a goal. They deny such concepts because they believe that history may not be grasped by superimposed points of view, but that the historical process itself must become the measure and goal of evaluation and so be capable of other points of view with contrasting significance; thus new methods of interpretation must be kept open continually. To the modern thinker, "the problem of resolving world order" appears to be an unattainable and unnecessary quest. Only in the recognition of the plurality and complexity of possible points of view and criteria for interpretation, does one think that he is able to deal with the historical in the second half of the twentieth century—an epoch extensively determined by late rationalism. The result is a confusing array of positions about which judgments must be made. Their inner logic should not be disputed in the process but, by necessity, cannot be the last word in regard to historical processes. Not least of all, we must mention the resulting methodological conflict of historical research. We also must mention the resignation over against the concern of wanting to or of being able to understand history out of a system of unified value concepts. Thus it remains for those who represent world-views (this avoids using the word "believer") to propose lucid future perspectives. They must have nothing to do with reality; on the contrary, the goal of this world-view and the ways which should lead to it certainly can be set forth as a utopia. However, a utopia cannot be thought possible or believable without the transformation of the present.

Actually, there is a hidden connection between Schiller's "concept of goal," directed toward world history as a whole, and those ideological programs that view the utopia itself as a legitimate part of historical political thought. Behind it stands the final expectation of an eschatologically envisaged fulfillment of all historical life at the end of time. One only needs to distinguish between Schiller's expected enlightenment of world history at the end of the age, and the "utopian programs" that are expected to attain this perfect end-time existence in some foreseeable future by means of their own thought and power. This particular variety of so-called secular or "this-side" eschatology is held to be possible in the various grades of world-views of diverse color. It believes in the perfection of the world on the sole basis of human perfection of the world. In contrast, religious eschatology, especially the Jewish-Christian, does not expect this perfection from the point of view of human presuppositions, but projects an intensification of confusion and error on earth, so that a divine action is necessary—only God can bring the world to its perfection. Within this debate, there is still a question as to which point of view is more "realistic." The faith of "realists" often overlooks the truth and reality of the world, while the Christian world-view often is qualified as "unrealistic" or as "feeding with hope" for "the other side."

Here philosophy of history comes directly into contact with theological problems. However it is certainly no accident that a philosopher such as Ernst Bloch, influenced by a Jewish-Christian horizon of thought, spoke of the "principle of hope" in a mixture of secular and theological conceptions and, in referring to it, a Christian theologian could reclaim for himself just this horizon of hope (Moltmann). These thinkers had in common the beginning point—the heritage of Jewish-Christian conceptions of time and history—which furnishes the framework for a proposed linear course of time and history. Within this concept, one always understands, or expects, an improvement or a worsening of human conditions of existence.

With the concept of "linear" time, we encounter that word whose meaning is so debated, but which has been so influential in Western Christian historical thinking—that basic given fact that, *a priori*, governs all the newer history of philosophy. In fact, it is well known that both Old and New Testament theology can be termed "theology of history" and that often they are presented that way. For the less expert, any concept of "history" and "historical thought" other than that of a course of events moving straight ahead is not possible. Yet we must give a short treatment here of other possibilities of thought that were known by the ancient people, and against which biblical thought stands out as being different. The critical reader may contend that these have very little to do with the philosophy of history, but actually, the starting points and presuppositions necessary for various views of history and concepts of history are present in such concepts of time. In order to present this difficult subject matter as concretely as possible, we will discuss very briefly some examples from ancient Egypt and Greece.

b. Excursus: Understanding and Reckoning of Time

One visualizes that since the earliest days, the course of time for humankind has been discernible in the change from day to night; the course of the stars; the change of seasons; the repeated cycle of the budding and fall of the vegetation; and finally, in birth and death in the realm of the human and animal world and in the succession of generations. Insight into these natural cycles of life brought the awareness that life takes place in constant repetition and that as a result, the world surrounding humanity is an ordered one, with the cyclical course of all natural beings completing itself in an orderly manner. A further step was taken toward the concept of "time" and the development of a feeling for time when one regulated, evaluated, or counted sections of this cyclical course. The beginning of such counting is in reality the hour of birth of the calendar.

In fact, we are able to say that the Egyptians, at least in regard to measuring the year, were in the forefront of those who sought to reckon time. Most important to them was the flooding of the Nile, which fertilized the soil, and it was only natural to begin the year with an event so important for continuation of life. Since the flooding of the Nile could not be fixed with regularity on one exact day which would be repeated, additional observation was needed for the creation of an extensively usable calendar. The knowledge of the heavens furnished a fitting guide. Near the time of the rising of the Nile, Sirius (the Dog Star), which the Egyptians called Sothis, was once again visible in the morning skies. For most of the year it could not be seen because of its late rising. Its reappearance fell, according to our present day reckoning, on July 19. With that event, the year had its beginning and was then divided into three seasons, each containing four months, with each month containing thirty days. Five additional days were added to those. The three seasons were termed the Flood time, Winter, and Summer. These reckonings were not perfect, since the year "calculated" according to these principles was a fourth of a day shorter than the Sirius year, which was the same length as the sun year. The Egyptians determined this discrepancy but had no measures available to bring these differences together in the "Sothis calendar" and the "common calendar." It was a matter of one day's difference every four years. Nevertheless, after four times 365, or 1460 years, the Sothic year would fall together with the common year, and this was generally known as the "Sothic period."

It is evident that these considerations for the bringing of Egyptian chronology into our calculation of time is of unusual importance. A presupposition for this, however, is the knowledge concerning which day on the common calendar the rising of Sirius took place. Such Sothic dates are actually known to us. We know that in the years A.D. 139–143, the common and the astronomical new year fell on the same date. By reckoning back 1460 years, one easily can attain the Sothic dates. However, to be a bit more certain of the exact dates, one must calculate the discrepancy between the Sothic calendar and the common calendar within a Sothic period, which involved a day every four years.

In spite of the difficulties in reckoning exact dates, this calendar constituted a pioneer effort, which was taken over by the Romans, and finally by the Christians. In two steps this calendar was improved and reformed. On January 1, 45 B.C., Julius Caesar introduced his "Julian" calendar and included an extra day every fourth year. Pope Gregory XIII introduced a "Gregorian" calendar in 1582, which brought about certain reforms. He ordered that in the years 1700, 1800, and 1900 the extra day should not be added, but that in the years 1600 and 2000, it should. Since this calendar reform was not introduced in all lands at the same time, there were discrepancies in reckoning certain dates, especially that of Easter. The Gregorian calendar was introduced in order to correct the errors of former calendars by advancing all dates ten days: October 5, 1582, became October 15, in the new dating. We will forego the process of converting the chronology of the old style to conform to important dates of the newer calendar—especially the date of Easter. But it should be clear that our calendar rests upon the observation and calculation of cyclical dates which had their origin in existential observations of the flooding of the Nile, and the Sothic dates developed from that event.

Nevertheless, we should take this opportunity to mention that, as everyone knows, the small unit—the week—made up of seven days, did not arise out of the larger unit of the year. It had a different origin. It is highly probable that it rests on an old Assyrian tradition, or perhaps an even older Accadian six-day week, to which a day of rest (sabbath) was added. One observed this day out of the fear that all would go awry if work was not halted. This division of a week, which had its origins in Mesopotamia, also influenced the Syrian-Palestinian realm and found its way into Israel and into the Old Testament. There, of course, a basic change took place in the concept of the seventh day. This seventh day belonged to the divinity and became a special holy day on which one rested in honor of God, even as God himself had rested after six days (Gen. 2:1-4a; Exod. 20:8-11). In addition, there was the conception that on the sabbath, one should reflect on the Exodus from Egypt (Deut. 5:12-15). Finally, the Jewish week was taken over by Christianity and by necessity came into conflict with the Julian calendar, which is still at work today in the rhythm of the weeks throughout the year. In contrast to Judaism, the seventh day was given up as a day of rest, and the first day of the week was made the festive day and later justified by the resurrection of Jesus "on the third day." The notable modern custom of lifting up Monday as the first day of the week and of placing Sunday, as the free day, at the end of the work week, does not correspond to either the Jewish or the Christian tradition and cannot be supported at all by the Mesopotamian calendar, because the day of the Sun god, Shamasch, which influenced our Sunday, could not very easily be put at the end of the week. Bureaucratic arbitrariness went beyond tradition; Monday as the beginning of the week is a sad monument to rationally managed time.

After these considerations concerning the principles and history of reckoning time, let us now return to our starting point—to the cyclical succession of the courses of nature. These observations could help develop the calendar division of time, but not a well-defined "consciousness of history"—at least not in the present Western sense. To be sure, the Egyptians could not loose themselves from the cyclical concept of time and conception of history. We still must address ourselves to further attempts in that regard. Basic for the Egyptian conception was not the idea of a unique course of development and the fixing of unique events on a line of time, but the conviction of the repetition of life and the course of all things related to it—thus in no way the "irreversibility" of all "historical." It is not possible here to trace or plumb the deep causes of such a nondynamic, or finally static, basic order of life and its relationship to reality. In principle, it must remain as it has been formulated by an Egyptian (with dictionary crispness): "The 'Egyptian' position in reference to history cannot be separated from its position to nature. History for the Egyptian is a natural event, and his concept of history concentrates on the discovery and execution of regularity, and places regularity in the foremost place of uniqueness" (D. Wildung [71:561]).

This is the principle that has brought about conflict throughout thousands of years of Egyptian history, causing statements of other forms of understanding to come into being. Yet even those forms must be evaluated in relation to this principle. Great stress is always placed on the example of the throne—that pronounced institution in the consciousness of the Egyptian people and state. In reference to the long list of its royalty, which in the later period was arranged into dynasties, was Egypt not able to develop a people with a high level of historical consciousness? The Egyptians did not experience it so. For them the throne failed to bring into realization a causal network of political historical developments, carried forward and acted out by the sovereigns as people of extensive foresight. Instead, each monarchy was viewed as a closed cycle, comparable to the natural cosmic courses. The ascension of the throne was a repetition of Creation; the so-called Sed festival signified the renewal of rule; the death of the sovereign brought an end to this rule but at the same time called for a new Creation—the repetition of that just experienced, but in the form of a new ruler. Thus there could not fail to appear what could be called a ritual for each monarch's reign—a course of firmly ordained orders under which the individual events were customarily placed.

In this connection there is a concept that is often used and that describes this ordained order of Egyptian life, although it is very difficult to apply to individual cases. It is the concept of *Ma'at* (m3^c.t), which can mean order, regularity, or truth, and in personal form, even can represent an independent deity. We can say with certainty that this concept was at home in the cycle of the Egyptian view of life and cannot be brought thoughtlessly into agreement with other presumed concepts of orders and laws that are rooted elsewhere. This is true for those one-sided attempts of more recent times to ascribe to the whole Near East a concept of world order that was generally widespread and that therefore may have influenced ancient Israel. Least of all can one begin to compare or equate the oft-spoken "righteousness of God" in the Old Testament with the Egyptian *Maat*. Here

distinctions emerge that cause one to take into consideration
various directions of thought.

Even in Egypt in the late period, one must consider the
fact that the static relationship of the throne to *Maat* had
changed. In the older period, there was a strong concrete
conviction that the ruler "actualized *Maat* in history." And the
ruler therefore was the only one who acted historically (E. Otto
[81a:65]). One understands, based on the background of most
recent Egyptian research, that the reign of an Egyptian could
be called a ritual, which sought its fulfillment in the
performance of *Maat*. Such conceptions were controllable
through inscriptions and presentations. During his reign, each
leader sought to accomplish a series of famous deeds such as
those that had been done by his predecessor, or at least to
document them as his own. Especially in the new kingdom, in
the second half of the second millenium B.C., each ruler allowed
the historical events and deeds of his predecessor to be
transferred over to his name—especially inscriptions on
monuments (Ramses II placed his name on a group of royal
images of the middle kingdom, in the city of Ramses). They also
took over presentations of expeditions and campaigns or
claimed for themselves a partial list of enemy cities conquered
by their predecessors. Certainly that has nothing to do with the
falsification of history, but rather with the pressure to
summarize their own reigns in a ritually perfect sense, often
within the framework of a very limited period of rule.

We must decline to list here the other consequences of this
Egyptian conception. However, mention should be made of
the fact that in the same degree with which the divine status of
the ruler was rooted in the fact that he was *Maat's* tool of
execution, he also was perceived as a person called to the
throne, even though in the middle of historical movements, his
worldly rule was viewed in its relative brokenness. Also in
Egypt in the new kingdom and in the late period, insights were
attained concerning the uniqueness and limitation of ruling, in

terms which begin to come near our own modern view of history.

From the belief that special events were locked in fate, there developed a consciousness of being unique, to which *Maat* no longer corresponded, and therefore could not continue to represent. In the turbulent transition period from the old to the middle kingdom (toward the end of the third millenium B.C.) there is a series of significant literary texts whose authors direct criticisms toward a creator god, suggesting that he may have created the world inadequately—otherwise there would not be unhappiness. In a very characteristic way, these words of reproach are intensified: "*Hu, Sia,* and *Maat* [creative utterance, power of knowledge, and order] are with you [the creator]. However you have brought upheaval over the land and the noise of uproar. Look, one strikes another; and one violates what you have commanded" (*Words of Admonition of an Egyptian Wise Man,* 12:12-13 [81:6]).

According to all that we know, there is no clearer way to explain a period of upheaval in Egypt. The cyclical symmetry is broken; the creator, rather than humanity must bear the guilt. He should have been able to foresee all that: "Oh, only if he [the creator] had recognized their character in the first generation, then he would have hurled his curse and raised his arm against them. His seed, their heritage, he would have destroyed" (*Words of Admonition,* 12:2-3 [81:6]).

On the other hand, it is in full accordance with the Egyptian basic view that certain expectations would be required of King Amenemhet I, at the beginning of the twelfth dynasty, in the middle kingdom, as recorded in the "Prophecy of Neferti." "Order [*Maat*] will once again return to its place, as soon as non-order is driven out." The ruler is the one in whom *Maat* is realized, and who therefore after the times of weakness and confusion is able to guarantee and create, in the sense of a creator, the "normal condition."

At this place in our deliberations, it is possible to take a considerable step forward. It has already been indicated that in the later phases of Egyptian history, beginning during the so-called new kingdom (in the second half of the second millennium B.C.), one encounters the greatest extension of Egypt's power under its most significant pharaohs. In addition to the traditional conceptions, a perception grew up that there could be a unique event of special, fateful validity. Concepts that pointed to a different understanding of time and history were used more frequently and consequentially, even if their origins in the cyclical image were not totally negated. Since the eighteenth dynasty, late in the epoch of the well-known "heretic king" Amenhotep IV—Akhnton—a word has gained in significance. The dictionaries like to translate it as "fate," but it actually means "determination," and according to more recent knowledge, its primary meaning is "a determined period of life." It is the word *š'it*, which according to the custom of Egyptologists is pronounced "sha-it." An example: It could be said of the great god Ammon of Thebes: "He lengthens the time of life, and he shortens it"; and then: "He adds to the fate of those *(š'it)* whom he is fond of" *(The Suffering Hymn of Ammon* I 350, III, 17).

"Life time" and "fate" appear here in parallel form. The "life time" of a human between birth and death, as it is measured to each person in the natural course of the world (insofar as it is connected with the cyclical principle of regularity) can be extended, in individual cases. The general attains a special form in the individual; the lengthening (or shortening) of one's life span is "determined" for the individual.

The section which has been introduced from the *Hymn of Ammon* teaches that the Lord of this "fate," or this "determination," is the deity himself—the one who sets the hour of death and the kind of death. It is not necessary to shore up this point with proof, but let us add that a comparison of the Greek *heimarmene* (in Latin, *fatum*) leads one to believe that Egyptian deities of the late period emphasized their superiority by being able to say, "I conquer the *heimarmene*. The *heimarmene* belongs to me." The Isis aretalogy of Kyme is to be read in this way when an already hellenized Isis is allowed to speak. The Egyptian Isis is held to be the mistress who grants life, especially in view of the uniqueness of human fate. " 'Isis', the one who grants life, the mistress of Philae, the one who lengthens the years of those who are devoted to her," is the inscription found on a large pillar of the Isis temple on the island of Philae in the Nile and can be dated in the Ptolemaic time.

Demonstrated finally in the consequent use of the different concepts for "time" that distinguish the unique from the "regular," is the growing perception that the decisive and unique moment is found in the recognition of cyclical courses. For this reason the statements of the Egyptologist Siegfried Morenz [76 and 77] are worthy of thought and lead to the conclusion that the unique moment is used in connection with persons and is expressed by the Egyptian word ' *t* (pronounced "at"). However the "time" that is set forth in a cyclical way, as presented in the course of nature and the cult and other pertinent orders, is represented in Egyptian by the expression *tr* (pronounced "ter"). For example, the following words stand in a mythical relationship: "He (god) has cut down the rebel in his time *('.t)*" *(Pap. Berlin* 3050, 3:6). There the subject is the destruction of world order: "At that time *('.t)* may it not happen" *(Urk.* VI, 124-5). The unique moment within or outside the cyclical whole is clearly marked by the concept '.*t* for "time."

In each case referring to cyclical processes of nature, time is expressed in a firm repeated rhythm: "In your time *(tr)* you have seen the Nile flood arrive" *(Urk.* IV, 498). In an inscription of a ploughing scene, one reads, "The time *(tr)* is good for great ploughing" (Lefebvre, *Petosiris* II, p. 21, Inscription No. 48:4).

One cannot dispute the findings of numerous other proofs by S. Morenz that the expression *tr* for "time" means time in its repetition, or geometrically phrased, time that can be represented as progress in a circular line. On the other hand, there is the time set for man—his "times" which finally will determine and constitute his "destiny"—all of which is represented by the term '.t. Therefore according to Morenz, it may have its geometric location in that unique direct stretch of flowing time as it is known to us today.

The critical reader may ask himself whether the geometric comparison which is reflected in the well-known use of the "linear" and the "cyclical" conceptions of time still can have exclusive validity for us in view of the Egyptian proof set forth in this area. Of course, it is theoretically possible to locate points of time on a circular line, or in reverse, to place circles on a straight line, or to join the two together in a straight line. Such geometric play demonstrates the limits of the comparison. For the final determination ought not be derived from purely theoretical possibilities of geometric presentations; the intended facts should be kept more sharply in focus as the actual starting point for these deliberations. It is a matter of two experiences of reality—two "times"—or better, two forms of time—in which man is encountered. On the one side he is bound up in natural processes and their repetition; on the other, he is an individual who is in control of the span of life measured to him and for whom "time" becomes "destiny," or "determination." Every man has "his time"—as profoundly as that might be understood. His time is a qualified time or as one has said, a "full time." It is not a time that man can have at his disposal in all abstract endlessness, but rather a time that the Creator has given to him.

It is certain that the Egyptians thought in terms of the cyclical course of time, that the ruler experienced and expressed the time of his rule in ritual form, and that the order of life was consummated in present courses in connection with *Maat*. The determination of the individual destiny is just as certain in terms of a firmly set period of life, the right moment, the uniqueness of the personal and "historical" hour. Such insights were adopted only gradually by the Egyptians in the long course of their history. Though if we compare the ongoing abstract mental processes in the realm of Western philosophy, we can discover a neutralization of the concept of time, set apart from its factual characteristics. The well-known and theoretical distinctions of the time of the Egyptians, emphasizing repetition and uniqueness, vanish into one concept of "time," which therefore must be redefined in each case.

Here one must look at ancient Greece, whose philosophical traditions had a formative significance for the West. What already has been said about the presentation of the relationships in ancient Egypt also applies to Greece. It is impossible to deal with such a subject in such narrow confines. Only a few indications can be given of important characteristics—especially those which can make possible a comparison with Egypt and the biblical circumstances. Very basic for our task is the fact that the gap between daily experience and intellectual control of the phenomenon in Greece was greater and more usually defined than in Egypt. In addition, the relatively unified form of intellectual-religious abstractions in the Greek realm were divided into numerous partial aspects according to their historical, religious, or philosophical location. This reflects the historical fact that the vessel of classical Greek culture is represented in various ethnic connections because of its appearance in many cultures. We must note also the geographical presuppositions—the mountainous nature of the land and the indented coastline, which caused the people to gather together in rather independent small groups, until they gradually found arrangements that were more comprehensive in nature. The richness of the Greek pantheon and Greek mythology is another expression of this fact. Thus we should not marvel that only at a relatively late date, did Greek thought attempt to become more "systematic," or said more conservatively, attempt to gather and compare the appearances of its world of experience and of the mind. This, however, led to confrontations, and to the discovery of conflicts and contradictions to which satisfactory solutions seldom were found. Exactly for that reason, Greek thought later was designed to help express this in further extraordinarily fruitful reflection. It is of deepest significance when Walter F. Otto ends his book on *The Deities of Greece* [82] with the conclusion that the Greek religions should be seen as not just "the faith of the most intellectual of all people . . . not just the glory of the living as viewed though the eyes of man. Rather their unique characteristic is that their clear vision is open to the eternal indissoluble conflict of life, and from this terrible darkness they received the majestic form of tragedy."

Behind these almost hymnic words of one extremely inspired by ancient Greece is hidden another fact that is evident to one looking from the point of view of the Orient. The relationship of the Greeks to their gods and their religion was very distinctive and less influenced by the numerous deities of the Orient than by the suffering that man must experience and from which even the gods were not free. The rich storehouse of Greek myths is almost impossible to comprehend and contains dramatic material expressed in both animated narratives and fortunes. These were available to Homer and influenced, in various ways, the myths of the West, including the libretti of operas.

That is the side of the Greek intellect that is open to the world. The other side is the one that lifted up the world of physical perception into the sublime heights of abstract conception and furnished forms of thought that still are applied in natural science as well as in philosophy. To the degree that this process became useful to humanity's own intellectual activity, the world of the gods did not lose its validity, but almost was absorbed into the primacy of abstractions, even becoming the object of abstract thought, divorced from the world of mythically endued stories of the gods with which it had been connected from the earliest times. Let us give an example here of the theme just discussed and offer further proof. We find a three-fold formula: "Zeus was, Zeus is, Zeus will be—O great Zeus." There is also an inscription on an image of Isis of the lower Egyptian Sais: "I am all, what was, what is, what will be" [78:482]. The connection between the world of the gods and an abstract conception of that which had been created—the present view and the coming reality—hardly can be shown more clearly than in this proof, which seizes on the philosophical premise in a direct dogmatic formulation of the divine essence "in time and eternity." A statement such as the following is understandable in its general significance: "Greek thought questions concerning the immortal essence within time" (W. Anz [63:531]). Of course, in this connection, "Greek thought" refers to that form of its intellectual activity which reached its high point in abstractions in the late period of Greek Hellenistic history.

Let us look back, for the purpose of an overview, and consider a few details that are related directly to our deliberations in reckoning time and the understanding of it in Egypt. Although Greece did not have the regularity of a cyclical process that could be deduced from a great river, it did share the concept of time as cyclical repetition. This is a widely held point of view, often supported by representation of time as a snake biting its own tail. The snake shedding its skin was understood as a symbol of rejuvenation. Closely akin to this is the thought of eternal youth, which also is represented as rejuvenation. These conceptions or others like them are apparent in other ethnic spheres as well. However, they demonstrate that the concept of a cycle should be deduced more easily from natural processes. The concept of temporal endlessness or "eternity" was not well known by the ancient people, as compared to the cyclical course, which was much more familiar to them since they observed it in nature. That direction of Greek religious thought which built upon mythical

ideas and incorporated "time" into its views of creation stood in
a certain opposition to such conceptions. *Chronos,* viewed less
as an independent god than as an element in creation, also
played a role in Orphism. There, next to water and the material
out of which the earth is made, we find *chronos,* which does not
age. In the *Hermetica,* the *aeon* is created, which then brings
forth the *cosmos;* this creates time *(chronos)* and this, then,
birth *(genesis).* Aeon thus is among the most difficult of
concepts because its closest relationship is to the cosmos, as
well as to the time working within it. In his presentation of
Greek religion, M. P. Nilsson repeatedly points out an
inscription at Eleusis which reads, "Aeon in his divine nature
remains always the same in the same and always keeps the
order of the world the same, which is and was and will be—the
beginning, the middle and has no end, having no part in
change. He is the creator of eternal divine nature in all"
[78:331]. This inscription alludes to consecrative acts at Eleusis
and demonstrates once again the epitome of unusual
abstractions; it is derived from the *Timaeus* of Plato. But it also
shows the logically inscrutable relationship between the
creation of the world and the course of time. Therefore, for
illustrative purposes, *aeon* is made absolutely into "the course
of the world." However it does not mean "the extension of
time," but the cyclical course of periods—especially world
periods, or "world year." Thus *aeon* also could be spoken of in
the plural, an expression which finally found its way into the
Christian literature. There, to be sure, it took on another
meaning under the influence of an Old Testament formula; it
cut itself off from the cyclical idea and suggested the impression
of "extended time." The New Testament expression "from the
ages to the ages" is an echo of the *aeon* conception of "eternal."
Repetition now meant the unendingness of a single time, in the
sense of "extended time" that flows from the darkness of the
past into the darkness of the future. Here already can be seen a
pertinent example of the reshaping of basic Greek concepts

under the influence of foundational ideas of "time" that are rooted elsewhere—especially in biblical, or more particularly, in Israelite thought.

In the Greek realm, philosophy lay hold of originally mythical concepts and made them the basic elements of speculative thought. Plato spoke of *aeon* as the ideal time, whereas *chronos* is the opposing image in the created world. Aristotle distinguished the two in a similar yet different way. He saw in *aeon* the timeless being of unchangeableness, but in *chronos*, the measure for variable movements. From this high point of such abstract and speculative thought, it is difficult to find an appropriate relationship to the empirical reality of history. For that reason the investigation here must include the way the Greeks expressed the unique in history, or more exactly, the way they perceived it. The unique is a breaking through of all of normality and thus must be viewed in opposition to the cyclical conception of nature. Logically, one could say that the unique is to be grasped as something special, or at times isolated, outside all order, and that it flows counter to the original plan. To be sure, the religious thought of the Greeks recognized a concept for fate, or more exactly, for "determination," very similar to the Egyptian use, which marked the imponderableness of human existence, the idea of *moira*. *Moira* originally was a deity who blessed, a founder, or a guardian of earthly order. She also effected upheaval and destruction. These negative features were attributed to her, without exception, by Homer. *Moira* signified immediate catastrophe, limitation; she brought an end to that which endured; she led to death—she embodied the necessity of death.

However, death was a limitation to the Greek gods; they struggled against *moira* in vain. In essense, the gods and fate were different. Only the gods possessed the ability to grasp an event that threatened to "go beyond regulation." For in contrast to humans, the gods had the ability to foresee events.

This force "beyond regulation" would certainly have "done in" Odysseus if Athena had not intervened on his behalf (Odyss. 5:436f). The gods could, to be sure, protect life as long as they were able, but at the end they were forced to give in to *moira*, which had set a limit for everyone—for everyone there was a "day of determination." The riddle of human destiny was played out in this conflict between the divine and the inescapable fate of determination. Also located there were the roots of the tragedy to which man is constantly delivered.

Of course, one must add that the thought that behind all determination, the divine will finally could be found was not foreign to the Greeks. Developments after Homer led in that direction. Solon can say, "Determination *(moira)* brings to mortals evil as well as good, and the nasty tricks of the immortal gods are inescapable" [82:279]. From such a perspective, one recognizes the attraction of a god who first was created in the hellenistic period and there rose to a higher significance—the Graeco-Egyptian Sarapis. In one of his aretalogies (second century B.C.) it is said of him, "I encase Moira" [76:77]. The power of a god was recognizable in changing or subduing the imponderables that seemed to be beyond the power of the gods to influence. Therein was the starting point for a complete theocratic order, which took up into itself the fullness of life and did not capitulate before "determination," but set its own goals and limits.

A side glance at the Graeco-Egyptian Sarapis gives us an opportunity to introduce a concept, *kairos*, which in the late hellenistic age took on special meaning. It characterized a point of time, the right moment, the decisive moment for development; but also a segment of time, or a certain limited time. It is evident that there one can see a concept that broke through the cycle of nature to bring about a unique development or set of events.

Actually, one can make the general statement that behind *kairos* was the Egyptian '.t concept. According to what has

been said previously, this indicates that the Greeks comprehended times and points of time that had meaning for the
individual existence of persons. A short overview of the
enumeration of human dealings that had "their time" and that
were brought together in the famous passage in Ecclesiastes 3,
can confirm this. The Greek translation of the Old Testament
made use of the *kairos* term throughout. Of course one should
take care concerning its understanding for the individual event
of history and its alleged unavoidable inevitability as
conditioned by *kairos* alone. *Kairos* does not work without
presuppositions but indeed, is bound to the very presuppositions that make it possible. Man is considered to have little or
no influence over these. The *kairos* is never the moment of
human decision, but a coincidence of earthly events and deeds,
made possible and accompanied by divine will. Ecclesiastes 3
brings out that very thing—man can do nothing when God is
not at work. He sets the *kairos*. For that reason, the *kairos*
concept was much closer to that of the divine decision of
will—in places it is very closely related to it. In a larger
framework, one could say, "Where there is no God, there also
is no *kairos*." Thus the favorite expression "*kairos* always
involves a time of decision" is only conditionally valid, for God
is the one who decides, or will decide. The self-constancy of
moira has been completely overcome. That means however
that *kairos* has little to say concerning the interpretation of
cyclical or linear time—just as little as '.t had in the Egyptian.
Thus, the "point of time," or the "segment of time," is
independent of a superimposed interpretation of cyclical or
linear time.

This question is a very enticing one: How, in view of the
Greek concept of time and finality, of fate and necessity, did
Greek historiography come into being? How could Herodotus
become the father of historiography, in the European sense of
the word? What convictions and factors directed the work of
Thucydides? We have named only two of the main representa-

tives of Greek historical writing. We do not have enough space here to treat the work of both men in any detail. Both in their own way were influenced by the basic principles of the Greek understanding of time and the world that we have just sketched briefly. Herodotus, in the powerful fullness of the colorful details he traced and shared, desired to show regularity and the human strength that determined it. In contrast, Thucydides worked under the pressure of the inner compulsion of all events, out of which necessities and failures resulted. However, finally these revealed a constancy that was related to the essence of everything human. Not accidentally, Thucydides preferred the political field for his observation, critique, and inquiries.

When we turn to the understanding of time and reality in the Old and New Testaments, differences will emerge between Egyptian and Greek thought—not in a diametric opposition, but in a subtle displacement of the accent, so that a distinct profile of the biblical world-view appears.

c. "Time" in the Old Testament

First of all, we can say that the comparison of Greek and biblical forms of thought is a direct classical subject of research. "The understanding of the Hebraic thought in comparison to the Greek" is the theme of a book by Thorleif Boman (1965). It is obvious that in such research, the question of the understanding of both time and space plays a significant role. Hebraic thought is related primarily to concepts within the Old Testament, but these also had an extensive impact on the New Testament.

Widespread agreement exists for the case that Old Testament thought, expressed predominantly in Hebrew and only occasionally in Aramaic, originally had no inclination to abstractions. After the postexilic period (circa sixth century

B.C.), abstractions increased and were used more frequently. Therefore it would not be very fruitful to begin with a systematic lexical study, or overview, of concepts of time in the Old and New Testaments; their significance must be determined from the interrelationship among the texts. One should examine not only the words for "time" and the related concepts in the framework of their context, but also the texts in their entirety in reference to the basic view of time that underlies them, just as their authors themselves experienced it. The methodological way suggested here is obviously simple but highly appropriate for its subject. A perusal of the dominant traditions of the Old Testament and the New Testament produces various points of view in reference to time and history. In view of the thousand years that separates these texts, no other result could be expected. As a regulating principle, one could offer what already has been set forth: the difference between a concept of so-called cyclical time based on natural phenomenon (signified often in the Egyptian *tr*) and the experience tied to the personal fate of an individual—a prominent point of time of fateful uniqueness (signified often by the Egyptian '.*t*).

The first words of the Old Testament and also of the Bible, standing as they do at the beginning of the creation story, are "in the beginning." They constitute a starting point of noteworthy certainty. Whereas other ancient oriental creation stories often start by giving a type of negative concept of the world, or by describing what was "not yet," or by attempting to describe "nothingness," or at least by naming a basic element from which the earth was later created, the Bible begins with the belief that the creation by God was "the beginning" of all that man could imagine. The elements of the work of creation appear in the second verse of the story, with obvious dependence on other stories external to Israel, which were largely of mythical character. Even behind the well-known "without form and void" (Hebrew, *tohu wabohu*) and the "great deep" *(tehom)* there are hidden mythical motifs or divine forms that played a role in Mesopotamian-Syrian creation narratives, particularly. In the biblical narrative they are demoted to mere physical elements of the future creation. The one Creator of heaven and earth triumphs over them, robbing the old foreign powers of their independent strength. The darkness of the primitive beginning is penetrated by the first act of creation—light. The question concerning the source of the light, as also of the stars, still remains open. God created the light and thereby limited the darkness—to be sure, not in a spatial sense, but rather in the manner of allowing a rotation between light and darkness to exist. In that way the first principle of temporal order is achieved, and as such is at once "named," meaning that by being named, it is brought into existence—"day" and "night." From this point on, the whole creation work of God is divided into days. It is only logical that the number of the days corresponds to the completion of creation. The world was created in six days and on the seventh day, God rested. This form of presentation is very different from a naïve primitive myth. Connected to the work of creation—to the division and filling of space with that which was created—there is a rounded-off unit of time. Thus there comes into being a seven-day rhythm, which becomes a principle of time for creation and for the world. It has been said earlier that the seven-day week had its origin in the Mesopotamian area, where it had been achieved by observations from astronomy. The details here must be based upon that fact. The Old Testament most probably adopted this principle of the seven-day rhythm, and it is well known that difficulties arose later in measuring the year because the number of weeks did not match the sun year. In any case, for the Israelite, the seven-day unit was begun with the creation of the world.

These few remarks give evidence of a double beginning point for the biblical understanding of time. The seven-day rhythm reminds one of a "cyclical" concept of time—a course of time characterized by constant repetition. However, this Jewish view had a "beginning," set by the creation. That seems to be the basis for a linear concept, or at least it could be so understood.

But the creation story does not limit itself to a seven-day scheme. In connection with the creation of the stars on the fourth day (Gen. 1:14), their explicit function is named. They are to designate and to make visible the divisions of time. They are to determine segments of time—"signs and seasons," "days and years." Here clarity is lost in translation. "Signs and seasons" could be interpreted more closely as "points of time and festival times"; "days and years" should not be understood exclusively in the calendar sense, but also includes greater realms of time of a determined order. Here the text demonstrates a striking ambivalence. Star-watching had become a very high art in Mesopotamia and often was associated with the "service of the stars" or even with the veneration of certain stars that were perceived to be tied to dieties. There is nothing of that sort in Genesis 1:14-19. The stars are stripped of such independent nature and made into functional supporters in the cosmos. Any reference to definite forms for reckoning time is also missing. Just as certainly as the sun and moon are named and the stars are added to them, there are no exact facts concerning a sun year or phases of the moon—perhaps in a polemical attempt to strike out certain predominate mythical astrological tendencies.

Now this story of creation (Gen. 1:1-2, 4a) is admittedly a relatively late text in the Old Testament and, in its final form, is postexilic. That accounts for its relatively high degree of abstraction, its reasoned thoroughness, and its theological clarity, in which the one God of Israel is set forth as the Creator of heaven and earth.

The well-known paradise narrative that is attached to the above, at least in its first verses (Gen. 2:4b-9), sets forth a process of creation that stresses the creation of man as most important. A much older text, it leaves out the "chronological framework" and makes no statements at all concerning time and the division of time. In the so-called curse (Gen. 3:14-19), the writer describes a world order that could be understood as cyclical repetition and outlines the nature of the circumstances that are to be allotted to men of all the ages. This description continues in chapter 4, which pinpoints the result of an order that has fallen apart at the seams—murder; but it also pictures the beginning of cities and the signs of an increasing "civilization." Of course, these events, strictly speaking, are conditioned by the cyclical concept. This is especially true, however, in chapter 5, where a list of generations is tied to a declaration of time; that test is typical of the author who already has spoken to us in Genesis 1, with his chronological division (characterized conventionally as the so-called Priestly Source). This fifth chapter continues "from the beginning," through the events of "world history," and up to the time of the great flood that destroyed humankind. Thereby a "historical" course is described—the decline of the first human race. That generation marched on to its destruction. One is uncertain whether, in this presentation of the narrative of the first human generations up to the flood and its consequences, an external source of "early human history" was used. At the conclusion of the flood, value is placed on the conclusion that God would never again allow such a flood to come upon humanity. The older narrative (the Yahwist) added the famous assurance in Genesis 8:22 that from now on, the natural rhythm of the earth would have no end, for there would be a continuation of "planting and harvest, frost and heat, summer and winter, day and night." The more recent narrative (9:1-17) has its climax in the same fundamental assurance, which is expressed in the so-called covenant with Noah. As a visible symbol of the promise that no other flood would take place, God set his rainbow in the clouds of the heaven and said that this would be an eternal sign for "future generations" (dorot olam). These are noteworthy concepts of time.

In other words, at a particular point in time, at the end of a uniquely arranged destructive flood, God spoke his promise to the whole human race after Noah—the generations (dorot) that would live in an incomprehensible span of time to come (olam)—a promise of unlimited maintenance of all natural order, with its own rhythm. The rainbow would remind the people of that promise. Therefore a new beginning is set before them—a declaration of continuing validity, related to the constancy of an absolute normality of a "cyclical" course in the "cosmic"—in the natural-physical structure of God's creation. In the moment after the flood, the "cyclical" is grounded and affirmed anew as the binding norm for all the ages. The act of the covenant with Noah itself bears the character of a unique divine assurance.

Chapter 10 does not relinquish this character of a "historically binding" setting; preparations are made for it at the end of chapter 9. For here, the "tablet of the nations" enumerates great personalities in the form of a genealogy of the sons of Noah, who are the primitive ancestors of the future human race. The names of the men from whom they sprang are identical with the designations of the most important races of people after the beginning of the second millenium B.C. This tablet of the nations has the character of genuine historical "information." Today, when the subject concerns the Semites, the Hamites, and (less often) the Japhethites—especially in the realm of language science—these names encompass nations or language groups within a larger realm, stretching from Armenia and Asia Minor, over Mesopotamia, Syria, and Palestine, to the area around the source of the Nile, that are named for the sons of Noah.

But once again the human race was compelled to surrender its arrogance because of the destruction brought about by the dissemination and the breaking up of the unity of

their language. The story of the building of a large city and of a
tower (Gen. 11:1-9) describes that event. However, this
rhythm of threats to human and world history, according to the
first book of Moses, reaches a turning point when a genealogical
line of men emerges out of the Semitic people, one of whom is
led into an unknown land. This man's name was Abraham. In
Genesis 12:1-3, it is said from him would spring forth a great
people, who would become a blessing for all humankind. If we
accept this unusual form of so-called genealogical thought as a
means of presentation, then this principle becomes the corner
stone of future developments, in the form of one individual. A
"promise" was given to Abraham, and promises call for
fulfillment. This scheme of "promise and fulfillment" that is
now introduced represents an essential category of biblical
thought—a category of time, which empirically demonstrates
the announcement and fulfillment of a historical way, or a
historical development.

Has the foundation been laid in this way for a linear
perception of time and history? One can say that insofar as one
views Abraham as the founder of the history of the people of
Israel, and as one observes that history as it continues into the
most distant periods, that a great dimension of the cyclical has
been introduced. The circle is completed when the promise
reaches its fulfillment. Thus the problem of the biblical
conception of time is demonstrated in its special magnitude.
Without a doubt, some historical facts are established with
Abraham and his descendants. In the promise set forth, a
fulfillment is awaited. In this promise, we also meet a division
of "time," which does not refer to "time" as an abstraction, but
as a fulfilled course of events. It involves a "destiny" of a unique
kind promised by God, and its fulfillment is subject to God,
even if man does have a direct share in it. In the conflict
between divine promise and the development of human
existence that the divine promise assures, life finds consummation. Israel also felt the direction of its God in such a way that in

the midst of that experience, human error was not ruled out.

This God of Israel, even as the Egyptian gods, knew his "time," and man can recognize it as God's right time, measured out to humanity. However, this God was not threatened by *moira*, and those that he protected did not need to fear falling into its grip. He held all in his hand. The God of the promise and of the way broke through "fate's" somber anonymity and gave to humanity the certainty of his presence. The God of Israel was not the God of Mount Olympus, in the circle of his fellow gods, who was forced to worry about fighting for the destiny of his human actors. It is God himself who sets the determination of things and "encloses *moira*," even as Sarapis did. Neither *moira* nor "fate" has a parallel in the Old Testament. The incalculable, which might appear as a force opposing God, has no place in the Old Testament. In this, the God of the Old Testament shows his superiority, for he is the only God who sets the norms and shows the way to his people. These norms bind his people, but at the same time, establish a safe existence for them in freedom.

Is this religion of the Old Testament a cleverly thought-out theory? Only a confused rationalism would so judge it. What Israel experienced with its God is in reality an "experience," or a certain maturing, but yet is a confirmed empiricism that has its roots not in a disposition to dialectical mental capability, but in a quality of experience not open to pure deduction. This experience was peculiar to the Old Testament authors and rested on the foundation of Israel's religious connections to its God. Only with difficulty can more be said. However, what has been said touches on the core of that unusual phenomenon— the people of Israel—which left its impression on the consciousness of the world and on the expression of the Christian faith in a unique way.

After this rather basic consideration, let us now return to Abraham's promise. That promise was actually fulfilled in the form of the people and the state of Israel. In this connection,

the date of the literary formulation of the promise is of
subordinate significance. Even if that writing first occurred
after the successful building up of the state of Israel, the basic
point of view still remained dominant. Even in retrospect, the
empirical validity proves that it is a uniquely founded principle.
In order to be in a state of relationship to promise and
fulfillment, means that in just these categories, Israel
understood it must evaluate and limit its "time." Thus "time" is
not meant in its abstract form, but as "time that has been filled
up by experience"—the event as the measure of the historical
conception of life.

It is part of the peculiarity of so-called Old Testament
historical writing that an event is not observed, fixed, or
considered because of its analytical historiographical significance,
but is viewed continually in reference to the unique acts and
settings experienced with God. In the course of Israel's history
and in its tradition, the promise had taken on a specific new form.
This can be alluded to here only in rough outline form.

The promise to Abraham is repeated explicitly to each of
the Patriarchs: to Isaac (Gen. 26:2–5:24) and to Jacob (Gen.
28:13). In this way there is a constancy to the divine promise
that extends over the generations and is affirmed and
established. Following the course of the Old Testament
presentation, one begins with the establishment of the people
of Israel in Egypt as set forth in the Book of Exodus. The call of
Moses to guide the Exodus from Egypt in Exodus 3:8 is
connected to one of the parallel patriarchal land promises, but
here it takes a different form. The subject is a land "which flows
with milk and honey," described as not being empty, but filled
with a host of people. In this we see reflected already the
historical situation which would be experienced later and
would make Israel's occupation of the land difficult. The goal of
the Exodus from Egypt always is expressed in that way. The
God who inaugurates, guarantees, and completes this development, allows himself to be questioned by Moses in reference to

the meaning of the formula "I am, who I am," which also can be translated, "I will be, who I will be." We will come back to this significant formulation, behind which is hidden a type of etymological explanation for the Old Testament name for God—Yahweh.

With the promising of the land to Moses we finally encounter one of the major themes of the transmission of the Pentateuch. Now the reader is put in a position of anticipation concerning the fulfillment of this promise; he awaits to see how Israel will reach this Promised Land, as well as enter it and possess it. Those events happened and actually are described in all their difficulty in the books of Joshua and Judges. That whole epoch, from Moses to the judges, is not characterized by any absolute data that would give us a closer picture of the situation. It may be that one would want to make use of the mention of the city of Ramses, in Exodus 1:11—in fact some do that very thing. That passage often is viewed as a reference to the erection of the residence of Pharaoh Ramses II (1290–1224 B.C.) in the eastern delta area, where the Israelites had been brought in order to help build the city.

The vague information concerning the age of some of the people who participated in this project is of importance in the redactive elements of the story. Moses may have reached the respectable age of 120 years (Deut. 34:7); Joshua, who directed the taking of the land, died at the age of 110 (Josh. 24:29). After his death, various persons are said to have led and "judged" the various tribes; their periods in office are described in the Book of Judges in various ways and altogether cover 350 years of activity. One should not preclude the fact that these numbers correspond to that rounded-off figure of 480 years, which seems to be at work here (I Kings 6:1). Just that many years after the Exodus from Egypt, Solomon began to build the temple in Jerusalem.

The exactness of these dates is not the object of debate here; the object is the marked disposition toward a periodicity

characterized by promise and fulfillment that is factually
supported and interpreted by exact figures. Indeed there is an
attempt to bring it into a more or less controllable chronological
structure. May that not have been in the interest of the oldest
times and traditions, in which such figures were missing? In
any case, a very decisive effort was made later to establish a
chronology, and "genealogical" means were used to a great
extent. If one takes note that a generation is described as
consisting of 40 years, then one can understand the later
tradition that Israel spent 40 years in the desert. That is an
assertion that could be oriented in the death of Moses as much
as in the generation that wandered in the wilderness. It was
said of that generation that it first must die before it would be
possible to enter Palestine (Num. 14:22-23). With Joshua, the
group that entered the land was delimited. The numbers taken
from the Book of Judges produces a sum of 350 years, and one
can add to that figure the 40 years of the wilderness sojourn and
the 40 years of Joshua's leadership, and thus attain the number
430. To reach 480, one needs 50 more years. These 50 years can
be obtained by looking at Joshua 14:10, where the whole period
of the taking of the land, from the time of the sojourn at the oasis
of Kadesh, is reckoned to be 45 years. Therefore the period of
Joshua gaines 5 additional years. Furthermore, in addition to
the 4 years of Solomon (I Kings 6:1), 2 years of rule are assigned
to King Saul, and 40 years to King David. Actually, the
enumeration will amount to 481 years, if one reckons on 40
years in the wilderness, 45 years involved in possessing the
land (Joshua), 350 years in the period of the Judges, 2 years of
Saul, 40 years of David, and 4 years of Solomon, up to the
beginning of the building of the temple (I Kings 6:1).

     In the 480 years, there are 12 generations, with 40 years in
each. That is also of the highest significance for an objective
evaluation of the tradition. Without a doubt, those who viewed
the period from the Exodus to the building of the temple in
terms of 12 generations were following an implied intention.

They considered the Exodus as the constitutive element for Israel's development, and 12 generations must pass before this God of Moses, the God who had led them out of Egyptian servitude, would allow a temple to be erected in the Promised Land. Thus one should view the 480-year figure of I Kings 6:1 as having originated in the perspective of Jerusalem. It is an attempt to round off the first decisive epoch of the life of Israel through the use of empirical facts. In the older traditions, the concept of the promise of the land was evident and understandable in itself. Later, the taking of the land was not viewed as a satisfactory completion of the earlier epoch of Israel; instead, the whole period, from the taking of the land to the building of the temple, was included. If one so desires, this can be viewed as an extension of the originally conceived cycle of "promise and fulfillment." One hardly can ignore the fact that in the cyclical idea of being "next-to-one-another," or coming "after-one-another," there is a hidden tendency to view time and history as linear. It is difficult to say whether this "linear" thought lay in the intention or only in the unconscious minds of the Old Testament authors.

This consideration is confirmed, but it also is complicated in a specific way when one becomes aware of more extensive "fix" points in Old Testament tradition. This can lead again to points of departure for a generally more free formation of periods of time, which also correspond to the basic thought of "promise and fulfillment." In the middle of the Pentateuch, or more precisely, in the framework of the Sinai event, which extends from Exodus 19 through Numbers 10, God concluded a "covenant" with the Israelites who were encamped at Sinai (Horeb), the mountain of God—a covenant mediated by Moses (main passage, Exod. 24:1-11). This covenant contained God's firm declaration that he would accept Israel as his people, but at the same time called for this people to be responsible in keeping his law. Expressed more succinctly, they were to follow a series of divine demands that had been transmitted in a

very broad and expanded way in the Pentateuch, beginning
with the Decalogue and especially concentrated in the Book of
Leviticus. The content of this covenant stood in correlation to
the declaration and promise that Israel is Yahweh's nation and
that Yahweh is Israel's God, as Julius Wellhausen has expressed
it so pointedly.

By no means was this norm binding only upon the
wilderness generation gathered at the mountain of God, but it
became the extensive foundation for the Israelite people.
Therefore it should not be surprising that in the course of the
later periods and traditions, other covenants similar to the one
made with Moses were concluded, which in part confirmed the
old tradition or added something new to it. Joshua concluded
such a covenant after he completed the taking of the land, in
reaction to the religious alternatives that were encountered in
Palestine (Josh. 24:15). Finally, toward the end of the period of
the kings, King Josiah carried out a distinct renewal of the
covenant in the temple of Jersualem (II Kings 23). An important
item here is whether such "covenant theology" is viewed as the
sole product of a later theory, or whether such "renewals of the
covenant" took place much more within the cult community of
Israel (the action of Joshua and Josiah certainly were not lifted
out of thin air.) Thereby, points of contact were found for
bringing Israel's life and relationship to its God into firmly
constructed courses in the sense of a logical temporal order.
Such covenant-making brought about reminiscences and,
through necessity, demanded a reflection of their own past, in
the sense of forms of life related to their present. These forms of
life were responsible to the old orders and were evaluated in
continuity with them. Very decisive, thereby, was the
conviction of the presence of God—one who was behind all the
orders and maintained them as valid, without any break. This
was both a responsibility and a guarantee for Israel.

The promise of the land and the covenant conception are
part of the most positive assertions concerning God that were

perceived as guarantees in the preexilic period. They are tied very closely to the history of Israel in the land and were supported by the prophets. The promise given to the prophet Nathan, in II Samuel 7, is related to the statement made to David that the future kings of Jerusalem would come forth from his family. In close relation to this are the statements concerning Jerusalem itself and its Mount Zion, that these would be considered as guarantors for the existence of all Israel (cf. especially Isa. 28:16-17; for the later tradition, see Isa. 2:2-4 or Mic. 4:1-3). Of course, mixed in with the traditional forms of positive expectation, one also finds warnings that place Israel's very existence in question. This is especially true of the indication of a coming "day of Yahweh," which would bring about something horrible that without exception would be confronted by the enemies of God (Amos 5:18-20; Isa. 2:11-17; Zeph. 1:7, 14-16); this last passage is the model for the Latin text *"Dies irae, dies illa."*

The final breakup of the Israelite-Judean existence as a state, which was occasioned by the fall of Jerusalem in 587–76 B.C., followed by the Babylonian exile, seemed to have brought about the end of these previous conceptions and orders. However, Israel could not continue to believe that. On the contrary, the certainty of the divine nearness and the declarations that once had been revealed to them experienced a grandiose renewal during the Exile and the postexilic period. Now, when the old orders of restoration were needed, they found an ideal expression. What the political realities of a land possessed by a foreign power would not allow, was now expressed anew in a valid promise that would be realized in some distant future.

They stood fast on Zion, and Jerusalem became the center of future activity. The temple was in fact rebuilt between 520 and 515 B.C. The hope that Zerubbabel, a man of Davidic descent, would be able to take over the role of political leadership, was not realized despite the soaring prophecy of

Haggai (Hag. 2:23). However, they were convinced of the fact that the promise made to David and his house had not perished, and that which had been formulated in the preexilic texts began to attain more support: God also had made a covenant with David (II Sam. 23:5; Ps. 89:29). Thus a Davidic covenant was placed with equal authorization next to the old covenant promises of the earlier period, whose explicit renewal was announced by Jeremiah (31:31-34). The Davidic covenant became the heart of the "messianic expectation." The concept of "covenant theology" was extended in still another direction. In connection with Genesis 17, the covenant promises given to Abraham were renewed and linked with the established custom of circumcision. The sacramental significance of the seventh day of creation was recognized in the primitive narrative of Genesis (2:1-4a). Thus it became institutionalized as a day of rest—a "sabbath"—and was even more strictly stressed.

From these details, it can be established that the understanding of time in the Old Testament remained very closely tied to divine promises. In the course of the development of the tradition over the centuries, life no longer could be possible outside that realm. In the maintenance of such continuity of traditional thought, especially in the period after the Exile, Israel found the strength to deal with its crises. The question could be asked, Where lay the roots of the Israelite understanding of its history, world, and time, as recorded in the traditions? An early thesis—one discussed very widely—has been set forth by Gerhard von Rad in his *Theology of the Old Testament*. This theory states that Israel, in its cultic celebrations, such as the festivals at the holy place, remembered its earlier history and renewed the covenant. In the rituals surrounding the king, the Davidic heritage was maintained, and in the cultic realm, the law from God's mountain was made present through liturgical means. Thus the cyclical repetition of the festivals became connected to the remembrance of the salvific acts of God. One might perhaps compare the festival calendar with its establishment (Exod. 23:14-17; Deut. 16:1-17). We can conclude there that Israel's history is a consequence of divine acts. This in turn created an Israelite "consciousness of history," and gradually, the perception of an ongoing linear concept of time. It is very difficult to demonstrate the details of that truth (we know very little about the oldest Israelite cult). Yet the core of truth in this thesis should not be ignored. At least one may have found a reasonable explanation for the gradual influence of Israel's understanding of time and history on the general consciousness. This was accomplished through the yearly festival, determined by the primitive cyclical concept and through the power of its "historification." Thus Israel's insights were deepened through the actual remembrance of moments in its folk history. This was not so in the area around Israel. There, to be sure, one could find the cycle of festivals in conjunction with the rhythm of the year. However the constitutive contents of the festivals were not the events stemming from the history of the tribe, or folk, but the vegetation cycle of the year. The greatest theme was the life and death cycle in the natural environment, embodied in the forms of various gods. One god or another died when the vegetation dried up in the summer months, but came back to life as soon as the rainy season restored the natural rhythm of seedtime and harvest. Marduk, Baal, Tammuz, and Osiris, and indeed, even Dionysius and Zeus of Crete were such "dying and resurrecting gods." However one can very easily mislead in saying that. One should not speak of a "resurrection" so much as a "coming back to life" that was granted yearly to these gods.

Israel had its harvest festival, and it also observed the course of the year, but it was very foreign to the Jews to allow their God to die—even temporarily. The God of Israel was not a God of nature and vegetation but a Creator of all cosmic powers. Above all he was comprehended as the God of leadership or direction, open to his people, and at the same time, determining their destiny. The battle against the fertility cults, as Israel encountered them in her neighbors, determined the conflict with the Canaanite expressions of the Baal cults and the Astarte cults especially, as witnessed to in the Old Testament. In fact, these religious forms did not constitute a declaration of faith that could be linked to the progression of time or to the destiny of the people. Even if the Israelite cult may have been connected to the annual festivals, and these then related to the remembrance of the early history of Israel, still the most decisive thing was not the cult, but the Jews' conception of their God. He approached them not primarily in nature and its orders, but in the completeness of life—in the sharing of his promises, laws and covenants. The cyclical nature of the cult was of service in all this, but it certainly was not the only influence in expressing a concept of history.

As we come to the end of the Old Testament period, the picture changes. In the apocalyptic forms of expression that already had been developed, a new complex of ideas emerged next to the older Israelite traditions. To be sure, the new ideas did not negate the principle of promise and fulfillment. For when they included the course of previous world history and the existence of great world kingdoms in their reflection on God's rule, and when they saw the end of this great political formation or awaited it in the imminent future, then hope was stretched out beyond empirically experienced history, to a situation of unusual idealism. The kingdom of "the saints of the most high," the "messianic age," the "thousand-year reign"— these were new horizons of expectation that were now opened, as concretely as they may have been imagined or presented. For the understanding of time, an impression was produced now, more than before, that the course of history was not moving in a cycle, but toward a goal—one that God himself had set—which lay outside all history but in relation to which all present "history" must be understood. Here we finally encounter the traits of an exclusive linear understanding of time.

d. "Time" in the New Testament

Now we dare to leap into the world of the New Testament, where apparently these eschatological components of the Old Testament and early Jewish thought became dominant. In connection with the preaching of John the Baptist, Jesus introduced his basic message of "repent, for the kingdom of Heaven is near at hand," in which one must understand the kingdom of heaven to be the "rule of Heaven"—therefore the rule of God. If this is true, then the impression is unavoidable that the message of Jesus was determined by "eschatology." He foresaw the end of history and the beginning of a new order of existence determined by God himself, however one might portray that coming situation.

Even though the message of Jesus seems to be totally immersed in eschatology—preaching that transcends space and time—yet one must reckon with the fact that "the message of the kingdom of God," based on apocalyptic conceptions of high spirituality, did not constitute the total preaching of Jesus. The Gospels do not always make use of that kind of language. They demonstrate in plausible ways, and in agreement with the expressions of the time, that the eschatological element was only one component of the expectations of that time. Since Jesus did not identify himself with the dominant streams of his time, but stood over against them in an independent way, it would have been highly unusual if he had granted a decisive authority to apocalyptic-eschatological thought-forms. In the Gospels we see a broad conflict with the traditions of the Old Testament, but less conflict with the teaching or attitudes surmised from contemporary Jewish theology. This must be formulated very cautiously because the expressions of Jewish theology in the time of Jesus do not provide us a firm teaching structure because of the difficulties of the tradition.

It is not inappropriate to view the message of Jesus as culminating in the demand to love God and one's neighbor (Mark 12:29-31), and therefore it is a valid renewing of the Old Testament tradition. Of course, there exists the major difference that Jesus believed that the forms of cultic-ritualistic piety were not sufficient (this is made clear in the Sermon on the Mount) and demanded both undivided loyalty to the promises of God and an openness to humans, recognizing the rights and freedoms preserved for humans by God. The arrival of the kingdom of God is reserved as God's concern, although it is possible for humans to perceive this kingdom if they place their actions under the promises of God. Jesus realistically confronted the volatile eschatology of his day and corrected the growing one-sidedness of the tradition.

Jesus himself did not bring about a great alteration of the understanding of time and history, but in the development that followed him, his teachings were added to the thought patterns of time. Thus the expectation of the kingdom of God became one element of a process that "accelerated" world history. With the thought of his return in the eschatological sense, Jesus took on features related to the whole world. His personality, which transformed man on earth and which was bound up in conflict, then gave way to the fullness of his superhuman, divine, messianic tasks. Jesus became a redeeming element in the eschatological drama, as described by Paul (I Thess. 4:14-17). The eschatological return of Jesus is made possible by the fact of his resurrection (cf. I Cor. 15) and by his fullness of power, which comes from his very nearness to God. We cannot deal further here with the fact that the theology of the apostle Paul, which was at work and is working in the New Testament, had a strongly normalizing power. However, his elevation of Jesus also transformed him. From the earthly personality emerged a transcendental-eschatological redeemer and world judge.

Since the return of Jesus as "a historical event" did not take place in the time of the apostle, it became necessary to explain this "delay of the Parousia" in a way related to the traditions. However, faith in the return of Christ was not fundamentally questioned.

We shall not trace the many-branched, complex further development of these thoughts; suffice it to say that one should remember the form of the Christian confession of faith, which foresaw a return of Jesus Christ at some distant end of the age: "He will return to judge the living and the dead." Thereby the eschatological Pauline component of Christian faith is viewed in an extended linear dimension. Our present world history is understood as a part of a "stretch of time" extending between Jesus' earthly wandering and his final return. As a result, the meaning of this history is determined by an understanding of the world that grows out of faith in Jesus Christ and that sees its eschatological fulfillment "on the last day." To that extent, "time and history" are fulfilled in Christian faith through the promise given to the congregation of believers—a faith expressed in the Gospel of Matthew: "I will be with you, even unto the end of the world." The meaning of our life in time is derived from the significance which Jesus Christ himself has given to his life, including all that he was and all that he said.

c. The Post-Easter Understanding of Time

From these basic convictions concerning the Christian understanding of time and the world, it is now possible to go back to the understanding of time in the philosophy of history, in the form in which it influenced European and all Western consciousness. In the "Post-Easter time" the understanding of time was oriented in the Christ who has come and who is expected to return again. Life found fulfillment in looking back on the historical appearance and resurrection of Jesus Christ. It found fulfillment also in the consciousness of his presence and in the hope of his return; in the sense of his eschatological role at the end of time, which grew out of the heritage of apocalyptic thought. As long as this understanding of time remained valid and undebated, the linearity of a "stretch of time," which moves toward an end, took on exclusive validity, and continued to do so for the believers in unbroken reality. However, it remains influential in the secular realm as well, even if the origin of this understanding of time, perceived in the letters B.C. and A.D., is obliterated at times today because of the intolerance of certain world-views. Some believe that B.C. and A.D. should be replaced with the apparent objectivity of a C.E. or a B.C.E., or something similar.

The validity of this Christian understanding of time, and the linear concept of time given with it not only is characteristic of the historical thought influenced by the Western world, but it also has experienced a corresponding historical-philosophical enrichment. For the original Christian understanding of time and idea of time had been shaped by the stance of faith and had been philosophically conceptualized. But it was robbed of its Christian character of expectation and anticipation in reference to the return of Christ and was made an independent formal category of thought by Kant, as an *a priori* form of perception of time, along with an *a priori* view of space. Since then, time has been understood as an indispensable characteristic concept of human thought. Without it and without the concept of space, nothing could be thought. Of course, one may observe that in substance, behind this philosophical abstraction of time, spoken or unspoken, the old biblical linear idea is still at work—a fact that is still recognizable, for example, in the modern "belief in progress." Such a view is instinctively goal-oriented, however one may think of this goal in isolation, whether one unceasingly strives for innerworldly technical or ethical-moral or social perfection.

If one wishes to separate "time" from this "thought of

progress" and address it in its own worth, then one must keep
in mind the theoretical possibility of the "return" and therefore
gain a basic significance for time in its cyclical form. A
world-view closely dependent on the thought of natural science
can hold that a cyclical physical concept of time is appropriate in
certain cases. The historian will dismiss it as unusable. Yet one
should not overlook the moment of truth that lies in such a
"rediscovery" of the cyclical. One only should be more distinct
in saying what one means when speaking of time. For this
undefined term "time" often does not betray, at first sight, how
it should be used. Time in a physical-technical sense, which
seeks to describe the thoroughly rhythmic-repetitive flow,
possesses a different "quality" than does *historische*" or
"*geschichtliche*" time, as has been discovered by historians and
by certain contemporaries. Basically, the old Egyptians were
correct when they spoke differently of "time" in reference to
natural orders and in stressing marked points of time in
reference to persons whom we are inclined to speak of as
"historical" (*historisch*).

Therefore one is not able to dispute the particular degree
of reality of either of the forms of thought that have been
brought together for descriptive purposes in a half-way
"geometrical form"—time as a circle and time as a line.
However, one last question presses itself upon the logical
mind—that of the content of truth in both methods of thought.
Is it possible to say which time is now—"absolute"—or does
this question concerning the essence of this form of perception
not exceed *a priori* all our possibilities? Must we capitulate
here to a phenomenon that also evades decisive speculative
thought? Under the new title "theology of history," one risks
the attempt to give a conditional answer. Before we end this
section devoted to the presuppositions of the history of
philosophy, let us make one last negative point.

The statements already made have allowed one to
recognize that there is no philosophy of history in the Bible, in

the sense of an abstract treatment of this theme. What can be said about "time and history" from the biblical point of view is bound up in the conception of "time filled up with events." Time is measured in terms of events, or better said, the event determines the time, starting with the natural orders of cosmic courses—days, years, and festival times. In view of humanity and its history, time is determined through acts of a divine setting—by moments of divine intervention, which open up new horizons of expectation. In our refined thinking, accustomed to abstractions, it is possible to question the ancient and biblical sources concerning their understanding of time. However, whether the answers the texts give, or that we attribute to them, would be the same as those the authors of these texts would have given concerning their understanding of time, is an entirely different matter. One might sharpen the question by asking, Can we, from our viewpoint, understand these old texts at all? However one should not overemphasize the "alienation" involved in this type of consideration. For even as we have just seen, within these texts a gradual change took place in the understanding of time and history—and to be sure in the direction of our own forms of understanding. In their summary form, as well as their individual form, these ancient and biblical texts lead us to different forms of human reality and therefore into a wealth of world-views. Such views often are influenced by our own abstract thought and its exclusiveness in treating conceptions that have become lost or overlooked by the so-called modern consciousness. The influence of natural science becomes valid at times in a one-sidedness that limits our horizons. This "exact" natural science that is under the influence of a materialistic world-view is removed from the philosophical categories and placed above it in the current canons of scientific categories, where an act must be proven to be valid. There, then is always the intention of accepting the science of "the intellect" only in a limited way. Man, however, does not live only by proven or provable empirical facts, but rather by perceptions, conceptions, and goals that have influenced him through time and history. In view of history, the often high esteem given to the factual fades away. It attains its value, indeed, "in its time," and the fact convinces us when "its time has come."

IV. Theology of History

There has been extensive preparation for this theme in the previous sections. If time becomes valid only in relation to the event, then we can trace the meaning of "time"—the meaning of that which we call history—only in the sequence and connection of events. For the "pure view" of time as a norm existing outside ourselves does not become available to us or help our perception, only "time" in relation to the events that we perceive can do this. In the course of the days in the birth and decay of organic life, the rhythm of life intrudes on us and takes on personal and human significance. This is due to the fact that we ourselves can be understood correctly only as living and thinking beings in time and at the same time within the chain of regenerations. Human life expectation is not limited only to the regeneration of its own kind; it does not remain bogged down in a biological model—although certainly this constitutes a part of human expectation. Moreover, individual life is sustained by the expectation of a "fulfillment," always according to design and presuppositions. The biblical basic conception of "promise" takes into account that the "principal of hope" is the secularized reflection of a basic problem of theology. However, "promise" is more than "hope," although as used in current speech, both seek to be fulfilled. For behind promise stands certainty—a guarantee—which can be given by the one promising. Hope is a form of expectation that is tied closely to the wishful thoughts of the one hoping, but it lacks certainty. It may be then that the object of hope itself can be grounded in promise. Then, however, hope would have pushed so close to faith that it already would be oriented in promise. We find this expressed in the grand summary of the Epistle to the Hebrews: "Faith is the assurance of things hoped for, the conviction of things not seen" (Heb. 11:1).

In the previous sections, our discussion has demonstrated that wherever the basic model of "promise and fulfillment" played a role in connection with the biblical concept of time, one already had confronted theological and deeply anthropological questions. And it is a fact that in these previous sections, we have spoken about circumstances that normally would be treated under the topics of "theology of the Old Testament" and "theology of the New Testament."

Both Testaments live in the realm where explicit stress is not placed on promises and expectations, but on hopes and fears that are kindled by the voice of God, from whence they receive their power and become the measure of thought, dealing finally with the content of the fulfilled life. It is certainly no accident that the Old Testament characterizes lax people and those who live a loose life or a rootless existence as "empty." This is no moral evaluation or insult, in the sense of "empty headed," as we use it today, but means a state of falling from the "fulfilled life"—from a goal-oriented human existence, which one knows to be bound up with traditions, education, and "social" forms. Here we should discuss the serious matter of the "lack of historical knowledge." For one should not understand lack of historical knowledge in an educational-pedagogical sense, but as a falling from the conceptions and supportive powers that are marked by faith and tradition and which mediate a sense of human community. Everyone lives within this community, by choice or not by choice, and one cannot separate oneself from it without danger to one's own existence. Atheism, nihilism, and anarchism are independently related positions which stand in contrast to the supportive and influential powers of the community. They lead without fail into an isolation that is not conquered even when one seeks to practice such world-views in a group. Strictly taken, the contruction of such groups is a form of replacement for the community from which one intends to separate oneself. The results of isolation are not inherent, but are in accordance with experience. They grow out of atheistic, nihilistic, or anarchistic views of the world which lead to intolerance and the will to destroy (even to self-destruction), but also to compulsive inconsiderate self-expression. Fortunately human nature normally opposes isolation and ideological oppression, whether intended or ordered. For that reason, natural opponents to these one-sided forms of thought continually appear and bring about the fall of the isolated, be it through direct or indirect resistance, in that the isolated one is smashed to pieces on his own position. There are sufficient examples of this.

This anthropological "fact of experience" leads by necessity to the conclusion that the human lives in a well-established narrow relation to time and history (sometimes he is not aware of it). He questions himself about the rules under which his life is fulfilled in time and history. Of course, these rules are limited, or we might say that there are many possibilities according to which existence is fulfilled and can be realized in time and history. "Biblical history" does not contribute to that distinct catalogue of norms nor can one be slavishly reconstructed. Evaluated very formally, biblical history has a "model character," in that it demonstrates and ponders positions and situations of human life and historical developments. Beyond that, however, as a part of human intellectual activity and religious experience, it is a part of "history" in its broadest relationships—that which unmistakably influenced, shaped, and even transformed subsequent history. Normative values can be deduced from it—values that are more comprehensive in scope than might first appear in the general admonition to love God and neighbor.

Theological and dogmatic reflection on the basic directions of the Bible has sought to comprehend the "structure of promise" that runs throughout the Scripture and that seeks to establish the way of God with humankind in a historical sense, from Abraham—indeed, from the creation of the world—to its last expressions in eschatology. One often speaks of the *heilsgeschichte* of the Bible. The extensive considerations developed in view of the *heilsgeschichte* of both testaments cannot be presented here. That would mean entering the realm of Christian dogmatics and so-called systematic theology. *Heilsgeschichtliche* considerations have their most important presuppositions, and perhaps also their most dubious weakness, in the fact that in a far-reaching way, they see the biblical canon as a unity that reliably reflects a type of historical progress, which is grasped as God's progress with man. At least that aspect might be traced in its broadest features.

One can see the *heilsgeschichtliche* concept emerging in the first pages of the Bible. God created humankind as man and woman in order to assure reproduction; and he allowed them to rule the earth; for they would have dominion over all (Gen. 1:26-28). God placed them in an ideal setting—the Garden of Eden ("paradise")—so that they might live there and tend the garden. However, in those first days they forfeited the good intentions of God by their own sin. The "command" not to eat from the tree that stood in the middle of the garden was given so that the limitless range of their perception might be hidden from them. This commandment was broken, and this trespassing brought about the problem of existence for future man: rebellion against God, opposition to his comandments, self-assertion, lust for all that appears possible before our eyes. The expulsion from the garden marked the unstable existence ordained for man from thenceforth.

From these basic considerations of man's "primitive

David or as the transcendentally
would exercise power—all these sh
chosen people in victory and defeat,
and security. He also assures
heilsgeschichtliche deeds and pror
things that threaten to cause his ped
wrongdoing. In such a way, one can
salvation through history—not a str
possible by repeated, regular inter
constant relation to the destiny of the
and therefore a way filled with
disruptions. Is it a way of ruin? Cer
not fall into ruin, because God up
purposes its unbroken existence.

The New Testament also stand:
for it has grown out of this "honor
salvation deeds of God. In relation t
appears as the mediator of a new (
Testament, with all its expression
concentrates on the basic elements (
that are related to humankind, and
the world. He points a way out
always-new offenses before God v
always burdened and because of v
with the loss of existence. We are no
the world is the judgment of the wo
out of this judgment situation must b
and that they are accepted before (

In this concept an unusually c
between empirical history—life a
individual existence. This is possibl
way because this "heilsgeschichtlich
offer itself alone as a "philosoph
receives its impulse anew from hi
extent, history itself actually has d

history," a *heilsgeschichtliche* bridge becomes possible and necessary. God must do something in order to liberate man from his condition—to redeem him from his "guilt," which has been a burden on him since the days of the Garden of Eden. Jesus' death on the cross and his resurrection signify the victory over the death that hangs over humanity (Gen. 3) and its fall into evil, as well as its opposition to all the divine promises, commandments, and purposes. Jesus won the victory over the serpent, which in many of the paintings of the crucifixion can be seen under the cross, defeated and impotent. All who turn to this Christ share in his work of salvation and experience the removal of their sins; for them, death is conquered in victory—all achieved for them by Jesus. At the end, they stand justified before their God.

This is the *heilsgeschichtliche* concept in its greatest dimension, in a form that the theology of the apostle Paul helped to mold. In the "Adam-Christ" parallel of Romans 5, Paul gave an impetus to a highly different form of Christian dogmatics. He himself contributed to its distinction and defined the form of the Christian faith with juristic terms and concepts, in order to assure the "justification" of sinners. It is hard to obliterate the impression that this "*heilsgeschichtliche* bridge," presented so briefly here, resembles a special form of "philosophy of history," rather than a "theology of history." Therefore it is not astonishing that Christian dogmatics, where it developed this teaching of justification very extensively and where it also made use of it anthropologically adopted very little from the Old Testament. For there we see indicated a way of failure that needs to be overcome. The beaming light of the Pauline theology of the New Testament appears to solve all questions and allows Jesus' earthly life itself and his declared message to fade into the background. For if the salvific work is grounded in his death and resurrection, then the life of Jesus—his wanderings and preaching between Galilee and Jerusalem—can be viewed as little more than a preparation for

his end. In this regard, one can obse
current Apostle's Creed, which goes
article, dealing with creation, to the
subject the redemptive work of Jes

Heilsgeschichte cannot and should
deep theological and anthropolog
salvation work of Christ in its best-l
knowledge of *Heilsgeschichte* must
the supportive foundation of faith and
Christ. However, there is still a diff
one thereby is touching on dimensic
whether there does not follow a dir
connection between the problems
appearance and suffering of Jesus as a
to understand this more fully, it is
Jesus' historical appearance and worl
back into such an extensive theologic
is given by that broad version o
understands God's work in Israel as a
having salvation as its end. *Heilsgesch*
present already in the Old Testame

The major cornerstone of Old T
has been discussed in connection w
The promise to Abraham, the promis
Moses; the Exodus from Egypt; the co
God; the entrance into the Promised
Davidic dynasty in reference to the
individual statements of the prophe
ued existence of Israel beyond the ca
of the temple after the Exile; the pr
(primarily as described in Jer. 31
renewing of the sabbath and circumci
of the world kingdoms that had grow
and the replacement of these with th
in which God and his "Messiah," be

"history" alone therefore is not its actual creator. For without that constant and intensive enduring relationship between humankind, who experience and endure history, and the certainty of the near and acting God, this way would not be possible.

At this point, we must point out two concepts of recent historical-theological work, which in their own way can help to reduce the perspectives. If, in view of the Bible, we speak of a "theology of history," then we have in mind that relationship just discussed which is unfolded in the conflict with the movements of political history and all its accompanying manifestations. For that reason, this history is not itself already "theology"; it does not have its own theological quality, because it is an object within the biblical canon. Even the fact of the tradition that transmits the individual events and the accompanying interpretations cannot be understood as an indication of the actual work of God. These are mediating processes. In view of the biblical traditions, only the basic conviction that the real God is truly at work in all history can be constitutive for theological knowledge. The theology of history unfolds itself not by a measuring of historical facts and their ways of being understood, but in that considered relationship that is accepted in the confesssion of faith—human history and divine action. God does not "reveal" himself through history, but he can be known in his divinity, in what we know as history. Such recognition does not have the value of empirical proof of the being of God, but the question concerning God, which is at work in man and will not let him go, is helped to become a continuous conviction of his present. A program set forth with the title "Revelation as History" threatens to consider only one side of the case—that history is very important for ascertaining God. However, history in itself has no quality of revelation. It takes on that quality primarily in those men who feel that they have been encountered by God in history or that in their histories they have experienced the historical way as the way of

God. From this experience, the Bible gives us plentiful witness. Its witness is able to awaken faith in God, who deals with man and therefore confronts him "historically."

The other way, more abbreviated in form, does not make use of *Heilsgeschichte* because the theological construction of *Heilsgeschichte* does not allow one to perceive the true way of God, but forces one to take note of the facts of history themselves—not some intellectual view imposed upon the facts. This type of consideration overestimates the degree of "historical certainty" that we possess concerning historical events, but underestimates the significance of theological-anthropological statements, such as are present in the concept of promise and fulfillment. It is a very important methodological conclusion that the factual nature of an event, and only a little of "history," has been transmitted, or is available to us, in a roundabout clear way. Therefore a relationship of conflict exists between the fact and its transmission. On the other hand, the form of the transmission expresses something of the depth of the experience, which is released in the ones affected by the event.

This perplexity, however, can take on theologically significant validity. It does not invalidate the causal connection of the factual; on the contrary, it makes it very interesting to the spectator and worthy of further research, for in that way the degree and extent of the perplexity can be measured. However, the factual itself cannot produce theological assertions, if it has not been witnessed already as "experience with the divine," or religious experience. For that reason, the transference of "historical-theological" insights to any processes of world history remains both a risk and a futile venture. Just the thought of possibly wanting to include a history of the revelation of God in the writing of a German, French, English, or some other history illustrates the absurdity of such an undertaking. This is not intended or desired by the representatives of the theology that is concerned with the facts of the history of Irael. Indeed they would like to separate the factual from the theological experience of the witnesses. Therein lies the beginning of a misjudgment, seen entirely apart from the question as to whether it is at all possible to make such a separation. This will be treated briefly in the next section.

With these last explanations undertaken, there is one final question to be considered and at the same time an answer emerges which seems to be at the actual core of a "theology of history." The question is whether, and how, God actually intervenes in history, and in what sense he is to be called "the Lord of history."

Expressed more simply, two basic external positions are possible. The first is that world affairs have nothing to do with the nature of God—that they are a human matter—an expression of human error and confusion. The other position is that God directs world affairs and that nothing is possible without him; the errors of humanity bring about failures in the development of history, which are either tolerated by God or, at times, regulated by him. Between these two extremes one may construct plausible intermediate positions, perhaps so that God holds the great developmental reins of humankind in his hands and therefore sets a distant eschatological goal for them. The detailed development of these goals is given over to humans, and there they unfortunately experience a negative decline. Humanity is able to progress upward from its deep points and times of need; this is shown by the fluctuations in the course of history, which are at the same time affected by the changing generations.

Such reflections leave one unsatisfied, because they proceed either openly or tacitly on the presupposition that there exists an objective supermundane decreed "plan of God" not fully accessible to humans, but which is brought to their consciousness in terms of their failures. In coarse words, one might say that failures are understood directly as the "punishment of God" in which human error is pushed into a close relationship with "guilt." Admittedly, such a "popular theology" is possible, and even widespread, but unfortunately it serves to bring general discredit to theological thought because one cannot or will not conceive of a "punishing God." At most he appears in such thinking as dark "fate," or as an enemy of humanity. We do not mention here that know-it-all who would like to abolish that image of God as a clever instrument for the maintenance of rule and dominance, as an aspect of some concept of authority to be overcome, or which already has been overcome. If one confronts such concepts with the biblical facts, one notices their one-sidedness, and certainly the danger of the scintillating half-truths hidden in them. It is self-evident that persons who are convinced of the reality of God do not view history as an open arena for the development of their own autonomous ideas; moreover, because they trust in God, they know the limits, but also the possibilities of human power.

For that reason, they will not evaluate human actions as being dependent upon a divine plan, but rather from the view of their faith in God, they perceive erring humanity, which is in the process of overstepping its limits. That happens usually when, in executing their own interests, humans are threatened, debased, despised, or even destroyed. The inclination to claim power cannot be rooted out; it brings about intimidation, lying, threat of force, and the establishment of clear positions on rights or ideology, along with intolerance. Unfortunately, in many cases these are the moving powers of history, but also the confusing ones as well. They are used by numerous men who, it is said, "make history," but history actually is written in the blood of the oppressed. It is difficult to believe that such fluctuation between striving for autonomy, power-seeking, and disparagement of one's opponent is the will of God. Of course, on the other hand, in reflecting on the susceptibility of human nature to power, one cannot take away the power of rulers without replacing it with something else. Even an association with power for the benefit of humankind must be learned. It requires insight into relationships, which is related to insight into human nature and its limitations and possibilities. In this relationship, faith can assume "the function of knowledge." It teaches one to understand his own nature, and that of others as well. At the beginning of his rule when Solomon asked for an "understanding heart" (I Kings 3:9), it meant that as a ruler, his primary desire was the ability to perceive divine, as well as human truth—insight into what is thought in the heart. It is interesting that according to the biblical concept, the Israelite "thought" in his heart, not in his head. The head as a symbol of intellectual capability is foreign to the Bible.

The "perception function of faith" (an idea stressed by Alfred Dedo Müller) includes insight into innerworldly relationships, as much as these functions can be mechanically transferable or taught in detail. The knowledge of God is not teachable. Under emergency conditions, the stranger to faith can be directed to the judgment of the believing. That is at the core of the statement that truth often is granted only to a few. Thereby involuntarily, we are brought again to the evaluation of the biblical sources. For they do not testify to "time and history" as objective forms of development, or to their factual nature in this or that sense, but they affirm the presence and reality of God, whom they have experienced. We offer one very important example of this. Moses accepted the task of leading the Israelites out of Egypt. In the course of a detailed scene, which becomes a dialogue with God, Moses asks this question (Exod. 3:13-15).

> "If I come to the people of Israel and say to them, 'The God of your fathers has sent me to you,' and they ask me, 'What is his name?' what shall I say to them?" God said to Moses, "I AM WHO I AM." And he said, "Say this to the people of Israel, 'I AM has sent

me to you.' " God also said to Moses, "Say this to the people of
Israel, 'The Lord, the God of your fathers, the God of Abraham,
the God of Isaac, and the God of Jacob, has sent me to you': this is
my name for ever, and thus I am to be remembered throughout
all generations."

From many perspectives, this dialogue is of exemplary
significance. The receiver of the divine revelation realizes that
his people will want to determine whether his subjective
experience is in accordance with an objective norm. In the
present case, the objectivity appears to be extensively
indicated, in that Moses can call upon the God of the fathers, a
state of affairs whose correctness is finally expressly noted.
However, there remains the pressing question, which
according to ancient thought was much more important—the
question of the name that would authenticate the existence of
the one encountered. That name is given here as "I am who I
am" or "I shall be who I shall be." The Hebraic play on words
set forth here in a relative clause (the verb of the relative clause
is the same as the verb in the main sentence) allows for both
translations. In spite of the complex discussions of these
"names for God," one can still say that "I am who I am"
expresses the constant present, as well as the future readiness
of God. Just as he is now both the present one and the true one
in conversation with Moses, so will he be also in the future,
when he actually leads Israel out of Egypt. One can correctly
presume that behind the Hebrew word for "I am" or "I will be"
('ahya) is hidden a more distant allusion to the Israelite name
for God, Yahweh. The identification of this Yahweh with the
God of the fathers is expressly affirmed once again at the end of
the story.

In a remarkable way, the scene shows the relationship of a
subjective experience of reality and the general validity of the
divine manifestation of self through revelation, or appearance.
The oppression of the Israelites in Egypt, a fact not to be

doubted historically, was ended by one man, who knew himself called to the leadership of Israel by divine disclosure. This disclosure was shared with him personally. The one disclosing himself was not just any voice, or a kind of subjective suggestion in the mind of Moses, but the God who had shown himself to be the God of Israel—this Yahweh who is also God of the fathers. In other words, God's reality breaks into a historical situation; he selects his man and equips him with full power; this completes what appears to be an entirely worldly act—the rescue of the people from their enforced labor. In intensifying this as a historical situation, God is "manifest" without history itself being called a revelation. In connection with the event, God is shown to be the one present. It would be superfluous to ask what Moses actually experienced. The author of the quote from Exodus 3 did not intend to compose a protocol of dialogue, but rather to introduce and present the fundamental nature of the nearness of God for the benefit of all of Israel, through the mediation of Moses.

That which is shown to be exemplary in Moses becomes just as valid for the prophets' experience of God. There, of course, at least on the periphery, one encounters the phenomenon of "erring faith"—men who come to the scene and claim to possess the message of God, but who do not have it. In contrast to the "false ones," another individual appears as the true prophet of God. Two narratives, one out of the early period of the kings (I Kings 22) and the other from the end of the same period (Jer. 28), are very informative. In the last instance, it is the prophet Jeremiah who still upholds the right, despite all the opposing endeavors of the prophet Hananiah. The events make it clear that the called representatives of the divine experience moved upon difficult ground when the object was to specify an exact point for the consequences of historical developments. Prophecy is great and unfailing in illuminating the circumstances of its own time. However, it reaches its limits when it is a matter of exact prognosis. Disappointment is also a part of prophetic destiny. The Book of Jonah is a good example of this.

These biblical observations are of special value in reference to the question concerning whether God is "the one who intervenes" or the "Lord of history." The fact that God is present in the affairs of this world does not stand open to question. However, how is this perceived? Here the spectrum of subjective experience or evaluation cannot be ruled out. For nowhere in the Bible does God appear in the greatness of an overwhelming gathering, in order to speak to humans. He constantly makes use of individual witnesses. It would be a somewhat curious analysis if one were to conclude, therefore, that the experience of God (somewhat in the sense of Feuerbach) is a subjective process—the simple projection of certain human experiential values on some imagined transcendental plain. That contradicts the biblical testimony in its entirety. For the God of both Testaments is the God who makes demands on humans, who contradicts them, and against whom humans chafe. Humans condemn this God, despise and reject him. In spite of his nearness, he is a God who is distant, who (as in the Book of Job) withdraws from the grips of humans. The experience of hundreds of years speaks in the writings of the Old Testament. In the New Testament, God's words appear in the mouth of Jesus as a message that separates the spirits—not as some pleasing invitation calling for the reconciliation of people to one another and to God, but as a challenging demand to the intellect. To see the Son of God broken on the cross, but then to hear his actual resurrection announced, and yet to establish faith and the conviction of the righteousness of God in those very events, produces an enormous contradiction that no philosophical system could endure. But it is in just this contradictory form that Christian faith can be experienced and that it can lay claim to being a historically grounded religion of revelation. One perceives that very fact in the relationship of the person of Jesus with the tradition taken over from the Old

Testament, as well as the consequent inclusion of Jesus in the Pauline theology's eschatological-Jewish horizon of expectation. Jesus was superior to and critically encountered every mere "spirit of the age." Does God intervene in history? He does—not in the spectacular form of a miracle that convinces the whole world, but through the fact that he prepares humanity for his reality and truth. The New Testament says to man, "You are the salt of the earth . . . the light of the world" (Matt. 5:13-14).

The object of the "theology of history" is not to research in the hope of finding a secret plan of God; to wish to find such a thing would be a bit presumptuous. Its object is humankind, which can conduct itself in a way appropriate to its knowledge gained in faith within the historical event only in a relative sense. "Faith" is not to be exchanged for the subjective piety of the individual, but is the sum of all his knowledge, deepened and enriched through religious experience. Such experience finds its orientation and its measure and certainty, but also its enrichment and correction, in the biblical witness.

B.
THE HISTORICAL IMAGES OF THE OLD AND NEW TESTAMENTS

I. Old Testament

This last section needs to deal with a question that by necessity has been produced from the discussions up to this point. It also grows out of the increasing mass of detail emerging from the progress of the exegetical and historical research in recent Old Testament and New Testament studies. Insofar as both testaments produce numerous words of the witnesses of God, from more than two thousand years of history, the question remains as to whether one can make trustworthy inferences from such testimony as to the actual course of that history. We do not possess any complete source for the early history of Israel up to the time of Saul and David, other than the Old Testament. Later, the ancient oriental sources become richer and clearer in reference to the relationship of Israel to its neighbors. Thus the question of control becomes easier as Israel is joined to the world of states of that time and comes into confrontation with them. Therefore, it is a question of how the Old Testament's view of the history of Israel and that of its neighbors coincides with the historical reality—a fact that by itself interests the historians. The clarification of this rather special problem helps one decide also the question as to what trustworthiness can be given to the biblical witnesses in the sense of "temporal-historical" certainty and controllability. Only then will relationship between history and theology become complete.

This complex of questions has been especially highlighted by the two volumes of Gerhard von Rad's *Theology of the Old Testament*, which examine the historical tradition of Israel and seek to single out its theological significance. One of the side effects of this understanding, brought about not so much by von Rad but by his readers and critics, is the increasing tendency to view the "historical picture" of the Old Testament essentially as a work of literary-theological combinations, and not as a correct reflection of an established course of history. The suspicion that the literary and theological formation of the Old Testament tradition may have had a strong influence on the "historical image" of Israel, as it once was known to us, has been deepened by the literary and historical research of Martin Noth. In his basic presuppositions, he accepted von Rad's results, but with certain modifications.

The problem can be clarified by a few thoughts set forth in von Rad's 1938 work, *The Form Critical Problem of the Hexateuch* which became the basis for his further work. He begins with a short text (Deut. 26.5b-9), which is clearly introduced as a prayer of the type the Israelite farmers may have spoken as they brought their annual offering of the first fruits to the holy place. It reads,

> A wandering Aramean was my father; and he went down into Egypt and sojourned there, few in number; and there he became a nation, great, mighty, and populous. And the Egyptians treated us harshly, and afflicted us, and laid upon us hard bondage. Then we cried to the Lord the God of our fathers, and the Lord heard our voice, and saw our affliction, our toil, and our oppression; and the Lord brought us out of Egypt with a mighty hand and an outstretched arm, with great terror, with signs and wonders; and he brought us into this place and gave us this land, a land flowing with milk and honey.

The farmer appeared at the holy place and offered up his gifts there with words that had their roots in the gift of the land. The individual farmer thereby understood himself as a member of his people, whom God had allowed to participate in that gift. It corresponds to the consequence of the so-called genealogical thought mentioned earlier. This thought sees the "people" as emanating from an "ancestral father" whom the farmer can speak of as "my father." The destiny of this "father" was threatened, so he went to Egypt and there became a great people, but was oppressed through hard service. God himself liberated them and gave them, along with the land, a strong foundation for existence, capable of bearing a great deal. The farmer recited this in the form of a grateful confession to God who had done all this for him and his people. Gerhard von Rad therefore called this whole text a "little historical Credo."

That this is a type of "formula"—a series of firm formulations in a definite sequence—is shown by the fact that the early history of Israel is presented in other places in the Old Testament in the same concentrated stereotyped way. It is not in the liturgical form of a confession, but in a lightly modified form, it still expresses the purpose of the salvation acts of God. This is the case in Deuteronomy 6:20-24; Joshua 24:2b-13; I Samuel 12:8; and also in poetic sections such as Psalm 136 and Exodus 15:4-16. A broader construction of the same scheme is found in Psalms 135, 78, and 105.

Now it is easy to recognize that the sequence of the main elements of this text corresponds exactly, or almost exactly, to the course of history recognizable in the Pentateuch, within the five books of Moses, or even beyond. There are relationships between the credo text as a concentrated "small unit" and the literary larger form of the Pentateuch that must be explained. Two possibilities are offered. Deuteronomy 26:5-9 may be the compressed presentation of the Pentateuch narrative, but known apart from it, and therefore may be a type of relatively late resumé of contemporary circumstances. On the other hand, it could be that in the "little Credo," and in its subsequent or parallel texts, we find the embodiment of the first "historical image"—the initial attempt of Israel to relate its early history to the taking of the land. This was done, one might say, for the purposes of worship—for the completion of a cultic confession at the holy place. In view of Israel's high regard for cultic tradition and transmission, which is the concern of numerous researchers and which is presumed to be in the oldest and original body of texts, it is understandable that von

Rad would see the core of the entire Pentateuchal tradition in the "little Credo." Therefore whatever develops in the cultic realm determines the greater presentation of "history" in the Pentateuch. From the roots of the practical cultic performance, there grew a "concept" of history whose formative elements were capable of being enlarged and were broadly developed in the Pentateuch. What appears to be a bit underdeveloped in the "little Credo," or not present at all, came to full completion in the Pentateuch. That is true especially of the earliest period. Thus von Rad, in view of the whole Pentateuch, could speak of an "expansion" of the history of the fathers (namely in the book of Genesis) and a "projection" of the primitive history (Gen. 1–11). M. Noth has attempted to soften these rather grandiose concepts that had been constructed concerning the growth of the Penteteuch. He does this by seeking the foundation of this process in a broad, professed, oral stream of tradition. However, in principle, he also holds firmly to the suggestion of von Rad, and many follow after him.

Now von Rad had discovered a noteworthy gap in the series of historical acts listed in the "little Credo." This is revealed even by the most cursory reading of the Pentateuch. The Sinai event—that meeting of Moses and the people at the mountain of God, where law and justice were proclaimed—is missing. This constitues the very center of the Pentateuch (the chapters of Exodus from 19 on, the whole Book of Leviticus, Numbers 1-10). This event was taken into consideration only in a relatively late text (Neh. 9:13-14). Following the logic that the "little Credo" is the core of the oldest tradition, or at least gives that appearance, von Rad viewed the Sinai pericope as an "insertion" into the historical arrangment traced out by the credo text.

Here nevertheless the historian must be quick of hearing. How, when, and why was the Sinai event "built into" the Pentateuch? Did it not belong there originally? Did the credo text perhaps suppress something (and why)? Did the Sinai scene have some other origin entirely? Was the mountain of God not directly on the way from Egypt to Palestine for the on-marching Israelites? Was it not likely that there in the loneliness of the desert, God undertook to speak to his people? Or was it possible that on the basis of some kind of circumstance whose details are difficult to recognize, the giving of the law was, literarily speaking, placed back into the desert period, so that the author of the presumably old credo text could know nothing of it? Is there not a type of arbitrariness present in the placing of the Sinai event in the middle of the Pentateuch—an arbitrariness that took no regard for the course of history?

These are the questions that must have grown out of a purely literary consideration of the Pentateuch and the high evaluation of an alleged old cultic tradition in the "Credo." If therefore "Credo" and Pentateuch are at the same time figures of composition—products of different traditions placed together with, perhaps, even different goals—here the taking of the land, there the giving of the law—then should not the question concerning historical truth be a burning one? On what, then, should we build our conviction of the God experienced in history? On the factual nature of history? Or on a "historical image" of cultic purpose and origin?

The problem becomes even deeper when one questions the role of the "fathers" in the credo or "the fathers" Abraham, Isaac, and Jacob in the book of Genesis. How were they historically related to the group in Egypt, who allegedly descended from ancestors who had been driven to that place? How can one conceive of that? Should we expect only "historical image" but no history? We do not have room here to deal in detail with this range of thought or to present arguments for and against the various views. It must be said plainly that no full unanimity exists among researchers concerning the determination of the relationship of these legitimate questions which touch upon the biblical text—if the word "unanimity" can be used at all.

If, in the following, an attempt is made to clarify the disparate views and observations in order to make the differences as well as the inner relationships of the problems just weighed more understandable, it must be added that this attempt cannot really help one form a judgment. Gerhard von Rad's opinion that the "little Credo" concerns itself with a very old tradition is problematic and has been long recognized as not fully supportable. Undoubtedly there are individual details present in the credo that have been redacted but not arbitrarily constructed, but which are supported by older, if not the oldest, traditions. The cultic prayer text, which takes on a confessionlike form and whose elements appear elsewhere in the Old Testament, is quite probably a later conception dating from the early period of history, after Israel had taken possession of the Promised Land. What appears in this text in chronological order—especially the tradition of the fathers and the sojourn in Egypt—also can be viewed as parallel developments. Israel reached the Promised Land from two different directions—from Mesopotamia-Syria in the north and from Egypt, or more exactly, from the reaches of the desert south of Palestine. The word "Aramean" in the credo is understood as an indication that the fathers—the ancestors of the Israel to come—were Arameans, members of a widely dispersed people who, in the second half of the second millennium B.C., advanced on the lands of culture—Mesopotamia and Syria-Palestine—from the Syrian-Arabic desert. That also would explain why the "fathers" and the people of the south still could have viewed Moses and his group, in spite of the geographical distance, as part of a more or less common nation. They belonged to groups of people who dwelled in the area of the Steppes on the fringes of the fertile lands of culture, and periodically they would march into those fertile areas.

Such a complex movement naturally is difficult to grasp in any exact historical sense. However, this complex period of occupying the land is one of the rare times in the Old Testament when narratives, reports, traditions, and persons were extant and known. Obviously, there was a decisive interest in preserving those traditions and in transferring them from the oral tradition into a distinct literary mold. Cultic confessions may have functioned throughout as an intermediate stage. One such has been preserved in a rounded-off, perhaps amplified form, in Deuteronomy 26.

That details of these oldest traditions of the Pentateuch, from the fathers to the death of Moses (Deut. 34), can be inserted into the movements of world history of that time (end of the second millennium B.C.), is attested to by witnesses outside the Bible. These affirm the historical realm of the Pentateuchal tradition and its trustworthiness. Basically, that fact is not questioned today. Only the details raise difficulties and remain the object of discussion. How were the patriarchal traditions related to the land of Palestine? How was the Exodus from Egypt, away from the city of Ramses (Exod. 1:11), connected to the building activity of Pharaoh Ramses II in the east Delta (where a residence was built)? These questions have been extensively explored, as well as explained and confirmed in many different ways. Information concerning this may be found in any history of Israel.

Against this background, it becomes clear that the "little Credo" recorded the events very sketchily, and consequently the missing Sinai events must not immediately provoke the inference that some arbitrary "insertion" has been made into the history. In fact, one should distinguish between the form and means of presentation of Old Testament tradition, and the possiblity of drawing historical conclusions from these traditions. Of course that is not a general statement.

The tradition of the Old Testament that is to be historically evaluated follows the rule of tradition, which also can be observed in operation elsewhere. The oldest material is found in pericopes that are very difficult to approach philologically (such as the song of Deborah, Judg. 5). The formation of

legends is broadly categorized in narratives, which appear in
the garments of dramatically constructed conflicts between
"main characters" and reflect older or the oldest history. To a
great extent, the patriarchal tradition, Moses and his time, and
many of the narratives and reports from the books of Judges and
Joshua belong in this latter group. Before the state consolidated, this form of tradition was the most widespread. The
emergence of the political and cultic institutions led to the first
recording of "historical" events, the production of annals, the
reporting of occurrences, and finally the production without fail
of written documents of administrative acts—these have value
as a source of the most direct type. This process began in the
Israelite period of the kings. The only thing missing, as it were,
would be the "original records." What we know has gone into
the Old Testament in a complex form. Yet archeological
research has brought to light very few administrative texts from
the Israelite period.

Still, the question remains as to whether the "historical
view" written down and established in the "little Credo," and
which has as its purpose the presentation of the Promised Land
as a possession given by God, is connected with other
"historical views" that extend into the premonarchical and
monarchical periods of time. Without a doubt that is true of the
presentation of the possession of the land in the Book of Joshua,
which, strictly speaking, gives only a part of that process, which
was said to have taken place under the leadership of Joshua.
The details are very complex.

The Book of Judges demonstrates an apparent consistency
in its presentation of discernible connections of individual
traditions. Israel was forced to defend its land against hostile
neighbors. These afflicted the wanderers, as we find set forth in
Judges 2:11-23, because Israel had deserted its God again and
again. The danger of being influenced by the Canaanite gods
also existed—especially the god of fertility, Baal. That, as well
as the difficult conflicts from time to time with hostile groups

are historical facts. Yet the distinct theological theme of the Book of Judges is the causative connection between the forsaking of God and the threat of punishment by war. With the beginning of the period of the kings, primarily with David, we begin to find reports of a high degree of certainty. However, even they are caught up in theologically determined, overlapping conceptions.

Since Martin Noth's book, *Uberlieferungsgeschichtlichen Studien* (1943), the conviction has been widespread, though criticized from many different perspectives, that the books following Deuteronomy—the historical books of Joshua, Judges, I and II Samuel, and I and II Kings—have been redacted. This redaction faithfully preserved the old individual traditions, but these were selected and reworked on principles related to the basic demands of Deuteronomy. For that reason one brings these historical books (Noth views them as parts of Deuteronomy itself) together under the title of "Deuteronomic historical work." Deuteronomy presupposes, in the sense of the "little Credo," that at least since the days of the wilderness, Israel constituted a united people. Historical probability does not support that. Israel acted as a united people, entered the land and possessed it as such, and lived out its life in unity under the law of God, the Torah. That unity corresponds to the exclusiveness of the people's worship of one God—"Yahweh"—who allowed blood offerings to be brought to him at only one cult location in the land. The ideas of Deuteronomy sometimes must be expressed in the theme "cultic purity" and "cultic unity." In addition to that, one must see Israel acting as one united people.

The "Deuteronomic historical work" proceeds true to these basic principles. In the Book of Joshua, we confront the impression of a united taking of the land and a division of the land for the whole people. In Judges the people defend that land. The hostile neighbors were seen as instruments of punishment, because Israel had looked toward other gods and thus did not live up to the principle of "cultic purity." The Deuteronomic measure is fully represented in the books of Samuel and Kings, where the institution of the kingship itself stood in conflict with the one who should be the actual king—God, himself. Therefore the institution of the monarchy in I Samuel 8, is understood as an accommodation to the stubbornness of the Israelites, who desired to have a king, like all the other nations. However, from that time forward, those kings found it difficult to exist in that conflict between the will of God and the political exercise of power. The whole tragedy of the reign of the first king, Saul, was viewed in terms of the belief that the "spirit of God" had departed from him. In spite of considerable difficulty of an internal political nature, David received relatively good marks because of his conquering of Jerusalem, which laid the foundation for that city to become a metropolis, and there the temple was built (the most important holy place, in the eyes of the author). Solomon stayed in good standing as long as he was strongly involved in erecting the temple, but he was placed in the twilight after he married foreign wives, for that meant the introduction of foreign cults into Jerusalem. The subsequent kings were almost all judged on how they related to the cult and whether they worshiped other gods in addition to the God of Israel. As a consequence, one of the most significant acts of the reign of Josiah, described in glowing tones, was the cleansing of the land from the extensive cult practices of the Assyrians (II Kings 22:23). Over and above that accomplishment, he concentrated the sacrificial cult (in the sense of Deuteronomy) at the temple in Jerusalem. The fall of the northern kingdom of Israel is traced back principally to cultic political errors (II Kings 17). Significantly, however, this historical work did not turn the facts upside down, in that it always fought against the monarchy. The continuation of the Davidic house of kings was promised by a word of God in II Samuel 7, and became the ground for the "messianic expectation," which always referred back to that dynastic promise and held that a repetition of the reign of David was possible, or even certain.

Indeed it is not wrong to say that the Deuteronomic historical work transmits a "view of history" that is oriented in principles; it would certainly be out of place to understand this orientation as a kind of ideological foreign influence. Under no circumstances were older sources violated. Rather they were simply chosen, ordered, and evaluated from overlapping points of view. If one accepts the fact that this whole historical work came into existence in the course of the Jews' Babylonian exile (and that therefore the great catastrophe of 587–86 was behind them), one is better able to grasp what is intended. In this historical work a significant attempt was made to explain the destiny experienced, through the failures of the past. The measure of that which is "false" in the conduct of Israel against its God involves the breaking of the principles outlined in Deuteronomy.

In no way is such a measure the expression of a definite, all too orthodox "piety." That which was felt afterwards—that which found living expression in this Deuteronomic historical work—became the fundamental conviction of the Israelite prophets. The prophets impressed on Israel that there was no guarantee of "salvation." Israel was not protected from every danger because it had its own God. On the contrary, this God had his special methods of showing Israel the right way and of forcing it to observe them. Practically speaking, it appears that the prophets in their time reproached Israel for straying from the way of God through unrighteousness, stubbornness, arrogance, false certainty, social offenses, and political willfulness. Expressed another way, the increasingly centralized and determined administrative and economic structure of Israel did not have a means of self-control. The influence of the state on the basic order of small farmers brought about a new morality which undercut the religiously fixed concept of justice. In the external realm, the state became a political football in the power plays of the superstates of the time. Israel was not militarily sufficient and thus was easily dominated. Even when the Jerusalem monarchy remained in power after the fall of the northern kingdom of Israel (722–21 B.C.), it could not help falling under the influence of Assyrian interests. The impulse of self-assertion hindered these states from finding rules for dealing effectively with crisis situations of a social or economic nature. Here and there the prophets demonstrated that they had in mind an inner reorientation, but only with difficulty, if at all, could this vision be fixed to a new "view of society" in a programmatic sense. They sought their orientation primarily in the relation of the individual and of the entire people to set norms, or to fixed basic orders, which were anchored in the will of God. There was a close relationship to the traditional law valid in Israel, which was observed in many complex ways. As far as we know, this law was imparted to the people principally in the teaching of the priests (Torah). Even the king had to take his orientation within the law and did not possess the freedom to set forth a law of the state that was different in any way. Israel did not recognize or understand any autonomous state law, for it did not hold any form of rule or government as absolute. The bearer of the power was one who was appointed by the prophets and acclaimed by the people as an honored person.

It is only logical that in such a structured basic conviction, the causes of catastrophes to the state were not seen as due to false principles of politics, but to the failures of individual persons, and this constituted the people—from the one bearing the power, down to the last "citizen." When the Deuteronomic historical work reproaches the kings, all Israel is involved, and no one has the right, nor is it possible to escape the guilt or to place it on one responsible individual. Israel had deserted its God, and no one was excepted from that indictment.

The "collective consciousness" rooted in such community thinking is of course very consequential, in that it did not allow a separation out of the individual, or the attributing of the responsibility to "the guilt of the fathers." That such a danger existed is proven by the polemic against the slogan then being used: "The fathers have eaten sour grapes, and the children's teeth are set on edge" (Jer. 31:29; Ezek. 18:2). The eighteenth chapter of Ezekiel especially emphasizes individual responsibility—not in order to determine the innocent, but so that each individual may bear his share of the guilt. The contrasting picture is the expectation that when all turn to God, accepting a common responsibility and doing this with inner determination, then God will be in the position to forgive all and to produce a blessed development for all. That is the presupposition and the consequence of the "new covenant" that God had in mind to make with Israel after the catastrophe (Jer. 31:31-34).

We can add only as an aside that this conflict concerning the guilt of the past in the exilic and postexilic periods took up considerable room in the Scriptures. The rather difficult book of Ezekiel offers examples of dramatic clarity, making use to a certain extent of highly tense symbolic language in chapters 16, 20, and 23. The whole *Heilsgeschichte* of Israel—all those acts of the past, including being led out of Egypt, which Israel was accustomed to speaking of as its guarantee of the future—were now reversed. Israel must turn out badly because it did not grasp the positive acts that God wanted his people to do. These are examples of a negative analysis of history, far removed from self-justification and a timidity before the facts. They lead to the abyss of radical "self-criticism" and a merciless uncovering of guilt. They are examples of self-reflection, which betray something of the (oft referred to) "dialectic" and enigmatic nature of all events—not empirical data, but a high degree of speculative forms resulting from a conflict with "history." That this conflict does not evaporate into abstract language, but emerged in the concrete form of images is due to Israelite thought and its methods of presentation. More to the point are the words of Isaiah, "But you have burdened me with your sins" (43:24). Later he says, "I have swept away your transgressions like a cloud" (44:22). Thereby a breakthrough is secured. Humans, recognizing that they are entangled in error, come before God as the ones about whom God has been "concerned." God is now the one who, according to the ensuing insight of humankind, can take away the burden that is on them. All that self-reflection—this is clear in its full range—is not entangled in logical-dialectical games, in the balancing of one's own maxims with unfamiliar ones that might be rooted in the autonomy of the human process of thought. No principle is softened or made relative. In the logical weighing of that which is thinkable, the conclusion is never reached that "God is guilty." The "Israelite historical thought" does not indulge in the inner logic of the inevitable "pressure of the facts" but finds the beginning and end of its thought in that point of reference that is called God—the God of Israel—at the same time this brings a personal confrontation with reality. By the term "personal God," we mean that humans becoming "historically" conscious of themselves do not see themselves in time and history as delivered up to one principle or another, but experience something "personal," which demands a personal answer. Israel's God is a person, not a principle. Therefore he is still just as "true" and constant, as variable and forgiving, after humankind has experienced his "anger" and been "turned away." The continuum of this Israelite view of history, which found expression in Deuteronomy and the prophets, did not consist in the continuity of a principle but in the constancy of a personal encounter, which became both a point of orientation and a guarantee.

Because Israel experienced its God in both destruction and advancement—in "wrath and grace"—it continually established a breakthrough to a new existence, to further thinking and living. Its historical images are so realistic because it recognizes the brokenness of all existence, as well as perceiving the continuum of the historical way. This is true also because both worlds of experience are present in view of that "principle" that really is not a principle, and in view of its relationship to the person of God, a relationship that constantly is being renewed. The promises to the fathers, the thought of the Messiah, covenant theology; or even more concretely, the promise of the land, and the hope of Zion; or finally, the expectation of a "kingdom," demonstrate that God is all in all. These are all figures of the horizon of historical experience that are not imagined but that have accrued to the people through history. This "historical data" is not theology nor does the revelation appear as "history"; rather, God is present in Israel's being, in its self-understanding, in the analysis of its existence, in its experience and hope. Of course, Israel did not experience its God suddenly—not in one event or act alone, not "directly from above," not in some punctual contact as the tangent of a circle—but in the growth of experience, in the development of its reality. The various traditions of the Old Testament testify in that truth. The New Testament wisely also testifies to it.

The "historical view" of the New Testament is certainly not portrayable in the form of such a process, as it was experienced in the Old Testament throughout the centuries. Indeed, one should ask whether and how the New Testament is joined to the world of experience of the Old Testament. Did not that "presence of God" in Israel, as especially expressed in the Old Testament in a personal experience with God, undergo an intensification in the person of Jesus Christ?

II. New Testament

One must keep in sharp focus the fact that Jesus was first heard by Jews; Jesus was first followed by Jews and they molded the traditions about him. Even Paul was a Jew and had to be convinced and "won over" by Jesus. On the other hand, Jesus was not recognized by the so-called official Judaism and therefore was rejected by it as the most personal direct representative of the God of Israel. This fact is alarming and almost borders on the irrational. For Jesus spoke the language of his people; he thought in their categories, lived in their holy texts, and did not appear as a militant absolutist leader of a group. In contrast, he had men around him in his so-called disciples whom he himself first had to train, to "educate," to convince. Yet it appears that they were not convinced, but left him after his death, or even before his death, in the hour of his greatest and final crisis. They constituted a community centered in a person—a fact which, sadly, is very hard to envisage. The master's death appeared to have resolved the cause he represented.

The spiritual and theological-historical system which Jesus experienced in his time was complex enough. He shared in it but even today he cannot be placed clearly under it. That appears to be a disadvantage, but perhaps it is an inestimable advantage. Jesus appears as a personality of unusual indepenence in all the brokenness of the tradition (for there are no writings of Jesus or any attributed to him), and yet he was experienced in all the streams of thought of his time.

All the questions concerning the origin of Jesus are removed from the realm of conclusive examination. That he belonged to the house of David and thus was of the kingly line, is attested to by Luke 2:4, where the line of Joseph is traced to Bethlehem and the house of David. The same is not said of Mary. From the viewpoint of the virgin birth, Joseph must be excluded, thus the Davidic origin of Jesus becomes problematic. This difficulty is seen also in the two different genealogical tables in the tradition (Matt. 1:1-17; Luke 3:23-38). Both contain the name of David, but nothing is said of Mary. The problem involved in the virgin birth was intensified by being associated with Isaiah 7:14 (Greek version), a messianically understood passage, but it proved to be an important part of the New Testament tradition (cf. especially Matt. 1:18-25). This problem took on even greater significance under the influence of the school of the history of religions. Mary's rank as the mother of the Son of God, or more exactly, "the one who bore God," placed her very close to other women who gave birth to divinities and who did not need the reproductive act for birth. An example of this is the Egyptian Neith of Sais. From an inscription on her statue as set forth by Plutarch, we learn: "I am all—what was, is, and shall be, and still no mortal has ever lifted my gown." Neith also is called a virgin [111:67]. In such association, the historian must place the otherwise noncomprehensible phenomenon of the "parthenogenesis" of Mary. Yet the influence of the formative forces of the tradition is shown in the interest in the subject, which is theologically conditioned. As an aside, one might note that Schiller's instructive poem "The Veiled Image at Sais" was inspired by Plutarch, among others [128]. However, the original sexual background was excluded in favor of the question about truth.

What remains is the negative conclusion that Jesus' origin is not explainable; also, his intellectual background is difficult to illuminate. He grew up in Galilee, far distant from the center of Jewish piety in Jerusalem, in a background of various ethnic and religious influences. It may be possible that these served as a presupposition for the fact that Jesus found undivided attention not in his native city of Nazareth, but in the areas close to the small cities influenced by Hellenism around the Sea of Gennesaret. There is proof that Jesus participated actively in the worship service of the synagogue (Mark 6:1-6; Matt. 13:53-58; Luke 4:16-30), but his education did not come from scribes or from other Jewish personalities.

His baptism by John the Baptist does not allow him to be placed in the group of disciples around John (cf. Acts 19:1-7), but does demonstrate a point of connection. "Repent, for the

kingdom of heaven is at hand," is the content of the message of
John and also constitutes the beginning of the message of Jesus
(Matt. 3:2; 4:17). That this message of the coming kingdom of
God was the beginning, middle, and end of Jesus' preaching is
emphasized again and again by the New Testament, as well as
by the research built upon it. The only debatable point is how
Jesus understood this kingdom. It is easy to think of the
"kingdom of the saints of the most high" (Dan. 7) when one
encounters this concept of the inbreaking cosmic end of
history. However, Jesus did not represent only this apocalyptic
component of the expectation of the end of time, which is for
the most part quite free from definite demands on the living
generation. Jesus viewed the kingdom as already here, or very
near, if a number of people were to do the will of his Father in
heaven. Following such presuppositions, he could say to a
scribe, one of the most highly educated Jewish aristocrats of the
period, "You are not far from the kingdom of God" (Mark
12:28-34). That example demonstrates a dominant emphasis in
the message of Jesus. He knew the theology of his day, but he
did not adopt it without reservation. He chose parts, reshaped,
and opened up new views not known before. For him the
kingdom of God was no natural event—no phase of the
end-time that depended only on God's own decision—but was
an event closely linked with the attitude of humankind, here
and now. Jesus broke off the point of a purely eschatological-
cosmic expectation and connected it with the well-known
demands of the Old Testament to love God and neighbor,
which one can recognize easily in the passage cited above (Mark
12:32-33). Thus Jesus did not do away with the Old Testament
tradition, but made it more radical in nature by concentrating
on central demands and making these into a norm. The first
chapter of the Sermon on the Mount (Matt. 5) shows this
through the detail of contrasting rhetoric. This unusual
intensification evident in the works of Jesus indicates that he
accommodated himself to the tradition, but at the same time

fixed a new goal for it. In that process, he relativized traditional elements, such as healing on the sabbath, expectation of the Messiah, and ritual laws. This brought him into conflict with the official position. As long as Jesus remained in Galilee, he was successful and essentially unopposed. The way to Jerusalem, which he realized was necessary, brought with it the great conflict—a head-on collision with the elite spiritual and political leadership. The "scribes" were composed of parties of various origin. The exclusive group—the Pharisees—preserved the tradition—especially the law and its interpretation. Jesus struggled with them and with others concerning the office of the Messiah (Matt. 12:35-37 and parallels). The Pharisees took the strict nationalistic approach of opposition to the Roman government and the hellenistic influence in the intellectual life of the nation. In contrast, the Sadducees, the ruling aristocrats of the Jerusalem temple, were close to the Romans and were open to hellenistic thought. Their realistic political views made them unpopular among the traditionalists, especially since they had opposing viewpoints. They rejected belief in angels and spirits, the Last Judgment, and the resurrection of the dead. For that reason, Jesus debated with them (Mark 12:18-27 and parallels). It is difficult to prove the often-accepted view that the Essenes, a very independent group, but very exclusive and open to Greek ideals, encountered Jesus or even exerted some influence on him.

We can conclude that Jesus functioned as a well-versed outsider, who knew the traditions, was tied to the society and oriented to the central theology, although critical of these, at times strictly rejecting the traditional attitude, diplomatically averting them, and transforming them into another concept. It is difficult to trace the sovereignty of this personality back to the all-surpassing *kerygma* of the early church alone; on the contrary, his personality furnished the means by which that church was enabled to carry out its redaction of the tradition. The right question is, How did Jesus understand himself?

The scientific answer to this quetion is overshadowed by the conflict concerning the age of the tradition. When one attributes the christological titles given to Jesus in the Gospels—Christ, Son of God, Son of man, and David's son—to the later tradition, the justification for all historical questioning is removed. Though if one seeks the presuppositions of such titles in Jesus himself, or possibly in the thought-world of his closest surroundings (Matt. 16:13-20), another picture is produced. In view of his critical conflict with the tradition, Jesus always could make use of the traits of various conventional designations, which he then adopted and connected to himself. The old observation that, with the exception of Acts 7:56, only Jesus himself used Son of man, is rather unique. Indeed, this title, although marked by apocalyptic concepts, has a higher, yet distinguishable expressiveness. It signified that representative of the coming kingdom of God who would bear human traits and who would mediate between humankind and God. It even expressed the thought that the Son of man, who became comprehensible on earth in Jesus, was the image of man as God originally created him. Yet we still have the question concerning the self–consciousness of Jesus—a very complex problem that cannot be cleared up historically. Especially, one should not rule out the possibility that Jesus himself had attained a knowledge of his being but that he spoke very little about it.

In spite of the often-expressed skepticism that a "Life of Jesus" is impossible to write, his personality and work adapt themselves without contradiction to the historical picture determined by numerous Jewish parties, and by the severe inner political and social abuses of a beleaguered Palestine under occupation by the Romans. The effectiveness of Jesus would be placed in question if his death on the cross had been the concluding chapter; the event of the resurrection opened up unexpected dimensions. Through that event, the historical Jesus was even more confirmed, and the Christian world was deeply marked by the faith that would transform the world and take away the fear of death. To the extent that the resurrection goes far beyond the actualities to provide a challenge to the historian, it becomes the touch point of the Western, or European, understanding of existence. From its influence on Europe, it colors the understanding of existence in the world generally. For the history of Christianity and its subsequent effects are not thinkable without the resurrection. It exercised an indelible influence on the consciousness of the world.

In a few words, we would like to concern ourselves with the complexity of this problem. That the dead are resurrected, that life can return to a corpse, that earthly man can conquer death, and as such return again, are impossible concepts that contradict all experience. Therefore the rationally oriented person opposes such thoughts, and rationally oriented theological studies seek to discover a rationally clear explanation. In that kind of approach, there is a basic presupposition that Jesus' resurrection from the dead cannot be supported historically. Even more, the effects of Jesus on the early community showed him to be the living One, and the first Christians interpreted that as "resurrection," as a continuation of life, and as the presence of Jesus. That Jesus did not in reality resurrect, but "rose" into the *kerygma* (Bultmann), or that with the resurrection of Jesus the "interpretation" was set forth that "the cause of Jesus goes on" (Marxsen), are formulations that have been thought out with all intellectual sincerity and sharpness of mind. They represent attempts to explain how such an unreal concept as the resurrection could have come into being and be made part of history. Is reality encountered in such a formula? Can the historian be satisfied that in that way he has explaind the deep-reaching effect of Christian faith as set forth in the pronouncement, "He is risen," which defies all experience and becomes the heart of the *kerygma?* The pronouncement was believed, and to insure that the cause went on, the Founder of that cause was surrounded with a wreath of narratives and was described as One who could have done nothing other than resurrect. Was the presumption made on the intellect any less then than it is now? Does Christian faith rest on historical fiction that is conditioned by a skillful interpretation?

The concept of "resurrection," or rather, of the rising of the dead or the awakening of the dead, is not foreign to the theology of the Old Testament and Judaism. Isaiah 26:19-20 and Daniel 12:2-3 serve in their own way as proof for the starting points of an Old Testament belief in the resurrection. It also found entry into apocalyptic thought, in the form of a collective resurrection of all the dead in the framework of the drama of the end-time, a resurrection that would insure a share in the coming reign of God for all men. To that extent the interpretation of the resurrection was not a concept conceived especially for Jesus or for the benefit of some appropriate formula, but has its origins in the general concepts of apocalyptic expectation.

Now it can be concluded that Jesus died on the cross and that his followers deserted him and scattered across the land. After a short undesignated interval, a Christian church came into being in Jerusalem, and persisted. Acts 1:15 mentions one hundred twenty men. What brought this group together? Was this a community of remembrance, which devoted itself to "remembering" the One who had died in order to assure the continuance of his cause? As incomplete or as idealized as the report of the beginning of Christianity might be, still one must explain what caused this community to come together. The preaching of Jesus and its effect before his death does not provide a sufficient cause. Therefore it is not just the effect of the historical Jesus that one tries to rely on when describing the formation of the church after his death. Between the death of

Jesus and the first Christian faith, the New Testament places—the resurrection.

As a rule, the origin and background of the resurrection narratives have been explained from the point of view of "faith in the resurrected One." However, how did that faith come into being? One might say it was through the incorporation of eschatological conceptions. It is possible to argue that the experience of the new and abiding presence of Jesus was so formulated that the eschatological event which stressed a resurrection of the dead was anticipated in the person of Jesus. Jesus was resurrected from the dead because in his person, the eschaton had become active in our world. God was exercising in Jesus what he had intended for all humankind at the end of time—the resurrection of the dead.

As plausible as this sounds, and as much as it reminds us of later arguments of Paul, the question remains whether, as pure thought complex, such an intellectually complicated utilization of eschatological expectations would have been sufficient to bring about faith in the "reality of the resurrection." Here is the weakest link of the chain of thought that we have spoken of. It would have us believe that it was very simple to accomplish the transference of the well-noted collective resurrection of the dead, as known in the eschatological tradition, to the individual person of Jesus. Certainly a traditional significance had been given to the words "resurrection" and "awaken." For that reason, the spiritual conception of a dead personality who had been well-known to all could not be understood as a partial anticipation of an eschatological act—even the resurrection of the dead. In the Pauline theology, where eschatological concepts take on a comparatively broader spectrum than in the Gospels, this eschatological reference to the resurrection may appear to be relatively unproblematic. What needs to be explained is not the later expansion of the thought of the resurrection, but rather its application to Jesus. How was a historical person, who had died before the eyes of so many, connected with the thought that he had participated in a resurrection? The most unusual thing about it all is that the concept of a collective resurrection was transferred to a definite personality, Jesus, within a historical framework—representing a historification and individualizaton of the eschatological expectation. It is difficult to imagine that a thought pattern that made use of only traditional concepts and expectations would have been sufficient. What was needed was an impulse—an event that could deliver the mediating and trustworthy value of experience. The event of the resurrection is removed from the realm of all examination, but the historical aspects of the event can be set within certain boundaries.

Let us begin with the obviously external aspect of the "empty tomb." Where was the body of Jesus? Was an attempt made to find the body so that one might destroy the faith in the resurrection with one blow? Nothing is known of that. Indeed, the idea that Jesus' body was stolen was set forth by the enemy as a purposeful lie (Matt. 28:11-15). That obviously presumes the fact that the body of Jesus could not be found. Here unconquerable difficulties are placed before historical inquiry. The narratives of the "empty tomb" are purely rationalistic subsequent interpretations of the resurrection. Is it so simple?

The New Testament does not describe the phenomenon of the resurrection. However the tradition of the Gospels knows with certainty that people found the grave empty on the day following the sabbath. According to the oldest report (Mark 16:1-8), the women fled from the grave and were silent concerning what they had experienced. The manner of presentation demonstrates great reserve. It is related to the effects of experiences that individuals had known. We are not able to go any farther into the inner core of the presumed event. In fact, these are reported personal experiences whose objective impulse is removed from every inquiry. However, the silent shrouding of the direct event here is much more eloquent than the attempt to make a detailed description of the phenomenon of the resurrection (as was later done in the noncanonical literature and because of its excess, was quickly demonstrated to be a product of fantasy).

The testimonies that belong to the oldest material about the resurrection are found in I Corinthians 15:5-8; there Paul includes himself in the appearances. It confirms the fact that individuals, as well as groups, saw Jesus—he appeared to them. What actually happened is left to the honesty and subjectivity of the witnesses. In this connection, it may be important that, according to the testimony of the witnesses. Jesus was not experienced as an earthly person—one who had returned in his bodily form; Jesus encountered them in his supernatural new form—his *doxa*, as the Greek text says. Therein lies a possible key for the understanding of the resurrection. The subjectively experienced appearances confirm the presence of the living Jesus. Even such experiences help us to understand the origin of Christian faith and the formation of the Christian community after the death of Jesus and give an explanation for the fact that it was not a mere remembrance of Jesus—not just a monument to the beginning of Christian thought—but rather should be called a historical, new, earth-shattering experience.

The main purpose of the present deliberations is to explain the effective significance that the resurrection message attained for the history of the Christian faith. It was not a secondary product of a highly theological associaton of tradition and concept; not a *"kerygma* which is believed" or an interpretation taken over from some alleged tradition. The event of the resurrection occurrence cannot be shown to be a historical fact nor can it be explained. Yet it is possible to historically distinguish that short period of time between the crucifixion and the development of the church, because an unusual tranformation took place. The men and women who knew Jesus experienced the fact that the one who had died such an insulting death, and who, according to the custom, had been placed in a grave chamber, now lives. These words confirmed the repeated appearances and became the constitutive point of departure for the Christian faith and life. The sharper and more unrelenting historical analysis of the sources attempts to become, without allowing itself to be disturbed by kerygmatic premises, the greater and more "unbelievable" the origin of Christian speech and thought appear, from the point of view of its weak historical roots. The message of the earthly Jesus and the conviction of his resurrection have lifted themselves above an uncommonly complex historical field, filled with many errors. The independent profile set forth by the New Testament tradition of Jesus places him sovereign over all other groups and is certainly a historical accomplishment of early Christianity. Its strength, however, is due not to creative speculation after the event, but to the testimony of eyewitnesses who experienced Jesus after his death and became convinced of his resurrection. In the resurrected Christ, they recognized their only Lord, the *kurios*, and the Son whom God had sent as the "fulfiller of time."

The concepts last used here point in a presumed dogmatic direction and have a strongly formulated effect. They are the main concepts of Pauline theology and as such, become the normative forms of expression for Christian thought and speech. The well-considered diction of Paul, which is filled with various formulations and which was accepted in a complex way into the liturgy of the church, is a result of the unusual concern of that "great apostle to the Gentiles" that the work and significance of Jesus be introduced into the Jewish and hellenistic intellectual world and faith. Paul systematically began to weave the form of Jesus into the greater associations, some of which he originated and some of which he appropriated. This is apparent in the letters he wrote to individual churches. Brought up and educated as a Pharisee, he was finally overwhelmed by the appearance of Jesus in that famous experience at Damascus (Acts 9:1-22; 22:3-16; 26:9-18) He then broke with the official Judaism of his time, but

remained attached to its basic ideas and sought to fashion the
form of Jesus into the far-reaching sense of an event
incorporating all humankind. For this educated teacher of the
law, it was necessary to examine thoroughly and especially to
clarify the position of Jesus within Judaism, particularly the
ways in which he might have related to the Jewish ceremonial
and moral law. If the Christian is called upon to fulfill the
Jewish law, is that simply a presupposition of his becoming a
Christian or of his being a Christian? These components of
Pauline theology, in their canonized-dogmatic form, gave
Christianity that presumed legalistic background which
reached its peak in the "doctrine of justification." Its
complicated pattern of thought has often obscured the
understanding of Paul's intended presentation of the liberating
power of the gospel.

The other dominant Pauline thought comes out of his
relation to eschatological conceptions, in which he attributes a
special function to the crucified and resurrected Christ.
According to his own experience, he is convinced of the reality
of the Resurrected One and reckons himself to be among the
main witnesses of the resurrection (I Cor. 15:8). The
Resurrected One is the ground and certainty of all Christian
life. Paul concludes; "If Christ were not resurrected our faith
would be in vain and you are still in your sins." For Paul, Jesus
is the first who conquered death through resurrection; he
anticipated what all humans will share in—the resurrection of
the end-time. Paul saw this end, however, as coming in the
near future. Within his own lifetime, during the beginning
stages of his work, he expected the return of Christ in all glory.
Christ, the eschatological fulfiller (cf. especially I Thess.
4:13–5:11), would lead all humankind to God. Paul was
convinced that, in Jesus, the future already had broken in, and
thus he made Jesus the key figure in the eschatological
end-drama. In that regard, he made use of the traditional
apocalyptic conceptions concerning the end of the world and

set Christ forth as the "first" of all the resurrected ones, who clearly would introduce the eschatological last phase (cf. I Cor. 15:20-28). This explains the unusual significance that Paul attributed to the death of Christ—or even more, the Resurrected Christ. In contrast, the early Jesus and his life and work up to the time of his death fade away and become almost meaningless.

Jesus left the exact time of the end of history, in the form of apocalyptic, in a relatively undecided state. For Paul, under the influence of the Resurrected One and his own personal encounter with him on the Damascus road, the end of history became an immediate expectation. Strictly speaking, the Pauline view of history is very limited, because it depended on the apocalyptic, actually ignoring history in its well-known dimension as the history of the world and its kingdoms. What remains to him is the near future expectation of Christ, who then would end world history. That did not prove true. Paul himself must have recognized that he would not be allowed to experience the end. Later he deliberated in what state he and the Christians would exist after their natural death up to the day of the resurrection (cf. especially II Cor. 5:1-10). Between death and resurrection, there would be an interim period, or intermediate state—one which was difficult for him to explain. In the later church, which proclaimed the hope of the resurrection at the grave, Paul offered no binding information on the state of man after his physical death.

In a remarkable way, Paul can connect both the legalistic and the eschatological-apocalyptic characteristic thought patterns. Neither pattern is fully developed. This is evident in the much-quoted passage from Galatians 4:4: "But when the time had fully come [literally, when the fullness of time, *chronos*, had come], God sent forth his Son, born of woman, born under the law, to redeem those who were under the law, so that we might receive adoption as sons [literally, in sonship]."

This difficult text understands the present world as the one acting under the "law." For Paul it is the world to which he belonged—one he had experienced as a Jew and one which he saw himself standing over against in historical time. This world time, however, had reached its limits or its "fullness"—it fulfills or is fulfilled. The coming of the Son of God indicates this fact. But according to the text, he does not appear as the eschatological Lord of the end-time, but places himself under the conditions of the world and therefore under the law. By the power of his perfected humanity—his coming in time—he can bring about "redemption" for humankind, who are living under the law. That means concretely, that they are accepted by God and are viewed as his recognized children.

In this text, after he delivers up time and the law, Jesus appears as the One who is able to conquer the law and time, in order to bring humanity into contact with God. In a more comprehensive manner this truth is expressed in the famous hymn in Philippians 2:5-11. If one compares these passages— the one from Galatians and the one from Philippians—with the other eschatological component as it appears in I Corinthians 15, a certain conflict is evident. The earthly Jesus, placed under the law, creates redemption for humankind. The Resurrected One, whose eschatological return is expected, introduces the perfected rule of God. One cannot overlook an inequality between the "legalistic" and the "eschatological" components. The question remains, therefore, How should the individual human conduct himself "under the law," or moreover in "time and history," especially since the return of Christ obviously has been delayed? The answer is missing in Paul. That causes many conflicts. For Paul knows that man, as long as he lives, cannot satisfy the law. However, that means that he subjects himself to even further conflicts at work in "time and history." For this reason the Christian who has become conscious of this relationship of conflict between facticity and demand knows himself to be bound to the "law of the spirit"—the spirit that makes one alive and free from the "law of sin and death" (cf. the whole connection in Romans 7 and 8). Therefore even now in this world and time, the Christian can be conscious of the liberating power of the work of Christ. That is the core of the easily misunderstod statement that Christian existence is "eschatological existence." It is a life fulfilled in the "right now" of the kingdom of God, but the "not yet" of its full existence will be experienced by the Christian only when the kingdom of God becomes a reality. This is not just "comfort from the other side," but the fact is taken realistically into account that "law" and "time" will continue to determine this world. In addition, we will come closer to a perfect conduct of life when we fulfill "the law of Christ" (Gal. 6:2). That means that in this present time of the law, where Jesus' word and work is perceived as valid, we are able to experience the full life that no longer recognizes the antagonism of "temporality."

The consequences of Pauline thought for Christian faith and existence of the church in the succeeding centuries were rooted in these suggested relationships. For the Christian knows himself to be in a direct responsibility to God, before whom he attempts to be righteous, but he is also in that eschatological straight line that brings him into an encounter with the return of Christ. Thus the present Christ determines our personal lives, but he also determines all of "time and history." The apostolic confession of faith knows of this Christ, "who sits at the right hand of God, the almighty father, from whence he will come to judge the living and the dead."

Conclusions: Historical Consciousness and Faith

In connection with these deliberations concerning Pauline theology, it becomes possible to draw some conclusions, neither extensive or exhaustive, from the complex relationships that emerge from the course of our considerations of the understanding and significance of time and history. For with the fall of the Mediterranean religions, which took place after the elevation of Christianity as the official form of faith, the self-understanding of man achieved a new foundation. The Christian religion was being more and more adopted and henceforth no longer was tied to various national gods permitted by the state. Zeus and Jupiter lost their value. In their place, Christ appeared as the one who towered over all other gods and became a binding power. It is not difficult to understand also that the ecclesiastical dignitary knew how to influence the power and politics of the state. Under the sign of the cross, the Pope (in the East, the Patriarch of Constantinople) was able to play a role in which it is difficult to distinguish between the spiritual and worldly exercise of power. The entrance of Europe into "world history" came about under Christian signs. It is a well-known fact that the Kaiser of the Middle Ages, along with the consolidated powers north of the Alps, came into conflict with the Roman papacy. This two-sided relationship of power was brought together in the formula "the Holy Roman Kingdom of the German Nation." The world-view of the Middle Ages was characterized intellectually by its own national development and at least partially in its function by the demands of Rome. The greatness of such a self-fulfillment of intellectual political power as a *civitas Dei* should not be evaluated as a failure in development or in construction. The consciousness of history can unfold itself in a national framework, but at the same time does not ignore the apocalyptic end-time conflict. Scenes of the Last Judgment, which usually decorated the cathedrals of the Middle Ages, give eloquent testimony to this conflict, into which the worldly rulers also are brought.

This extensively experienced, uniform world-view broke up, at the latest, in the period of the Renaissance. The prevalence of nationalistic concerns and the emergence of the independent interests concentrated on humanity and the possibility of its development, brought about the end of that which would be known later as the Middle Ages. Among those factors, one also would include that feeling of a new time which, as everyone knows, loosened the relationship between the concepts of religion and morals. Man lays claim to his rights and made his demands in a powerful way. The movement of "humanism" is captured in its very name and finds even greater expression in the word "rebirth," or Renaissance. The separation from Rome that Luther desired did not lead to an extensive reformation of the Catholic church, the result of the Reformation was the division of the church. The connection of Protestant Christianity to the princes of the land was intended originally to be a positive one, but in the long run it brought forth only a weak reflection of the *civitas Dei*. The warring parties of rival princes, though very far apart on matters of faith, could give up the battle over confessional points of view and devote themselves to helping determine questions of power. The Thirty Years' War in Germany left the nations lame and allowed confessional interests to fade out of the scene in favor of political ones. The emerging absolutism characterized a new era, which prepared the way for nationalism. Philosophy cut itself off from theological-spiritual premises and brought about an Enlightenment of the mind, in which the autonomy of human logic was most important. Opposing streams of church groups did not fail to appear. The powerful attack of the Jesuits was directed primarily against Protestantism. The orthodox exegesis of the theology of the Reformation was always too concerned with itself and thus grew stale. This in turn produced spiritual awakening in the forms of Pietism and Methodism, just to name a few, and these gave a new impulse to Christian activity.

Still the national states formed themselves together into power blocks; the consequences of absolutism awakened the

historical Credo," but only in view of the land that had been promised and attained. Another greater and more broadly inclusive relationship was noted in the section concerning conclusion of covenants—at Sinai, at the assembly at Shechem by Joshua, and during the rule of Josiah at Jerusalem. The historical connection of land, monarchy, and covenant was renewed as a supportive conviction that affirmed tradition during and after the Exile.

We cannot spend enough time here on the significant role that Jerusalem played in the postexilic period. Jerusalem appears in numerous prophetic works and supplies the form and material for the entire historical work of Chronicles. Apocalyptic comes to grips with world history and awaits Israel's ideal rule under the direction of God. In this way a framework was established in which it became possible to address the external dimensions of time. In Jesus' concept of the kingdom of God, present and future confront each other. In Paul, under the influence of apocalyptic framework of conceptions, the kingdom expectation is moved from an imminent expectation to a future hope. In this constant renewal of its tradition, Israel gave an account of what it had experienced and kept itself open to the horizon of promise. The New Testament lives from the same basic ideas, which are finally extended into the distant future to the return of Christ.

The discovery of continuity that was accomplished in biblical history and that was supported by the conviction of a God who sojourns with man, is of absolute paradigmatic significance. The history of Israel and the way of biblical theology are difficult to reconstruct; yet it becomes even more clear that, in this way of spiritual and theological self-ascertainment, there is an example of what constitutes and supports humankind. It is a consciousness of the supportive ground in the living community in which the human stands, in which the individual's destiny lies, but which also is bound up with the expectations and hopes of the ethnic-political groups to which one belongs. In antiquity, such groups worshiped the same god, or gods.

Ethnic affiliation (in order to avoid the difficult concept of peoples, or nations), state affiliation, and cultic-religious connection, separately and jointly, constitute the guarantee of the tradition. All these help the individual to bring about those continuities in which he stands and lives. Consciousness of history is therefore not only knowledge about continuity, which each creates for himself in some way or other, but is also tied to institutions which themselves are very indebted to the tradition. In these institutions humankind finds both a foothold, a connection, and a direction. For that reason, historical consciousness is not oriented in theorems, but in facts set forth through institutions and their representatives.

To find one's way back to a historical consciousness therefore, one must accept the bonds that have grown up, and the means must be made available for serving the continuum of development in all openness for change. In a modern state, institutions guarantee the continuation of intellectual development, in order to bring it to reality for the general consciousness. Indeed, historical consciousness is mediated to the same degree by institutions of education, by churches, and by responsible governments. In regard to the European relationship, we can say that the European tradition is placed inevitably in the continuum of the so-called Western, or occidental, cultural traditions, which have marked both speech and thought. Its forms of thought have grown up from theological and philosophical presuppositions, but they also have received their respective nationalistic stamp. Thus every European nation recognizes the continuum of its history, which has been nourished openly or latently by those spiritual powers that grew out of the religion of Christianity and that have been and continue to be represented in the church. To that extent, in direct contrast to the organizational forms of the state, European historical consciousness is bound up in the religious-anthropological forms of understanding of life and history and is indebted to biblical thought. To build up historical consciousness, therefore, we must analyze critically the accrued forms of western European history, along with the history of its ideas and changing institutions. In order to escape a "lack of history," we must comprehend as a part of ourselves the heights and depths and especially the difficult phases of the history known to us. We must recognize also where the experience of error lurked in our previously shaped existence and spirituality. If correctly understood, historical and national consciousness are not instruments of might (they are often misused), but compose the necessary framework of intellectual self-discovery and self-realization. To say it very simply, history is a part of home.

Another point that stands out in these deliberations is the question concerning the focus of historical consciousness. In historical consciousness, we are not concerned with the details, which in their fundamental relationships remain unclear at times even to the researcher, but with concepts of history—those connected forms or thought complexes that can be comprehended. Nevertheless, the Old Testament does not deny that history can be interpreted in various ways and therefore can be expressed in different images. Its history has been understood in various ways in the course of the ages. However, in the course of changing historical insights, it still grasps the complex contribution of the direction of God. Even the history of the European people is very difficult to comprehend, and German history alone, in view of the last hundred years, has many different interpretations as we demonstrated in the introduction. Historical consciousness, therefore, is not to be confused with one logically exclusive "historical image," but in its varied expression it demonstrates its power and opens up new forms of understanding for social and political existence in time and history. The role of religious self-understanding cannot be separated from political decisions. On the contrary, political action also can be responsible to the depths of religious conviction. The *civitas Dei*, like the kingdom of God, is an ideal entity and is latent in earthly life—in life "under the law." Such insight grants a provisional character of transmitted power to every institution. Better persons are called to serve such institutions. To sound out the depth of biblical theology does not mean to seek some comfort for the next world, but to drain from time and history all the existence that can be gained from them—following the "law of Christ" and putting it into practice. In the completeness of our present dealings we are "not far from the kingdom of God." These words of praise were spoken by Jesus to the Pharisee (Mark 12:34).

Bibliography

The numbers in the text correspond to the numbers below.
(E.T. = English translation)

Preface:

1. G. Bonwetsch, H. Kania, F. Schnabel, *Geschichte der Neuzeit,* Nachdruck Genf, n.d.
2. R. Buchner, *Deutsche Geschichte im europäischen Rahmen: Darstellung und Betrachtungen,* Darmstadt, 1975.
3. F. Heer, *Quellgrund dieser Zeit. Historische Aufsätze,* Einsiedeln, 1956.
4. H.A. Jacobsen, H. Dollinger, *Hundert Jahre Deutschland, 1870–1970: Bilder, Texte, Dokumente,* Berlin, Darmstadt, Vienna, 1969.
5. H. Jahnke, *Fürst Bismarck: Sein Leben und sein Wirken,* Berlin, n.d.
6. Otto Kaemmel, *Deutsche Geschichte,* Dresden, 1889.
7. B. Kumsteller, U. Haacke, B. Schneider, *Geschichtsbuch für die deutsche Jugend,* Leipzig, 1939.
8. G. Mann, *Deutsche Geschichte des 19. und 20. Jahrhunderts,* Frankfurt /M., [11]1976.
9. J. v. Pflugk. Harttung (Hg.), *Krieg und Sieg, 1870–71: Ein Gedenkbuch,* Berlin, 1895.
10. H.U. Wehler, *Das Deutsche Kaiserreich, 1871–1918,* Göttingen, [2]1975.

A. The Encounter

I. Historical Research

11. H.M. Baumgartner, J. Rüsen (Hg.), Seminar: *Geschichte und Theorie: Umrisse einer Historik,* Frankfurt /M., 1976.
12. A. Erman, *Die Hieroglyphen,* Samlung Göschen Bd. 608, Berlin and Leipzig, [2]1923.
13. H.G. Faber, *Theorie der Geschichtswissenschaft,* Munich, [3]1974.
14. B. Faulenbach, *Geschichtswissenschaft in Deutschland: Traditionelle Positionen und gegenwärtige Aufgaben,* Munich, 1974.

15. J. Friedrich, *Entzifferung verschollener Schriften*, Verständliche Wissenschaft, Geisteswissenschaft, Abt. Bd. 51, Berlin-Göttingen-Heidelberg, 1954.

16. G. Fohrer u.a., *Exegese des Alten Testaments: Einführung in die Methodik*, Uni-Taschenbücher 267, Heidelberg, 1973.

17. L.H. Grollenberg, *Bibel-neu gesehen: Arbeitsweise und Geschichte der Bibelwissenschaft*, Stuttgart, 1969 (E.T., *A New Look at the Bible*, 1969).

18. H.W. Hedinger, "Historik," *Historisches Wörterbuch der Philosophie*, ed. J. Ritter and K. Gründer, Vol. 3, 1974, pp. 1132-37.

19. W. Helck, E. Otto, *Kléines Wörterbuch der Ägyptologie*, Wiesbaden, 1956.

20. E. Hornung, *Einführung in die Ägyptologie: Stand, Methoden, Aufgaben*, Darmstadt, 1967.

21. O. Kaiser, *Einleitung in das Alte Testament: Eine Einführung in ihre Ergebnisse und Probleme*, Güterloh, ³1975 (E.T., *Introduction to the Old Testament*, 1975).

22. K. Keuck, *Historia*, Emsdetten, 1934.

23. K. Koch, *Das Buch der Bücher: Die Entstehungsgeschichte der Bibel*, Verständliche Wissenschaft, Vol. 83, 1963 (E.T., *The Book of Books*, 1968).

24. Ibid., *Was ist Formgeschichte?* : *Methoden der Bibelexegese*, Neukirchen, ³1973.

25. B. Meissner, *Die Keilschrift*, Sammlung Göschen, Bd. 708, Berlin and Leipzig, 1013.

26. Ed. Meyer, "Elemente der Anthropologie," *Geschichte des Altertmus: Einleitung*, Vol. 1, Darmstadt, ⁶1953.

27. J.M. Miller, *The Old Testament and the Historian*, Philadelphia, 1976.

28. M. Noth, *Uberlieferungsgeschichte des Pentateuch*, Stuttgart, 1948 (E.T., *A History of Pentateuchal Traditions*, 1972).

29. G. Posener, *Lexikon der ägyptischen Kultur*, Wiesbaden, 1960 (E.T., *Dictionary of Egyptian Civilization*, 1962).

30. R. Rendtorff, *Das überlieferungsgeschichtliche Problem des Pentateuch*, Beihefte z. Zeitschrift für die Alttestamentliche Wissenschaft, 147, Berlin, 1977.

31. K. Sethe, *Vom Bilde zum Buchstaben*, Leipzig, 1939.

32. C. Westermann, *Genesis 1–11*, Erträge der Forschung Bd. 7, Darmstadt, 1972.

33. Ibid., *Genesis 12–50*, Bd. 48, 1975.

34. W. Wolf, *Das alte Ägypten*, dtv. Bd. 3201, Munich, 1971.

II. Portrayal and Hermeneutic of History

35. J. Bright, *Geschichte Israels: Von den Anfängen bis zur Schwelle des Neuen Bundes*, Düsseldorf, 1966 (E.T., *A History of Israel*, London, 1972).
36. H. Cancik, *Mythische und historische Wahrheit*, Stuttgarter Bibelstudien 48, 1970.
37. P.J. Cools, ed., *Geschichte und Religion des Alten Testament*, Olten und Freiburg/Br., 1965.
38. F. Dexinger, *Das Buch Daniel und seine Probleme*, Stuttgarter Bibelstudien 36, 1969.
39. G. Fohrer, *Die Propheten des Alten Testaments*, Bd. 6, 1969.
40. A.H.J. Gunneweg, *Geschichte Israels bis Bar Kochba*, Stuttgart, ²1976.
41. S. Herrmann, *Geschichte Israels in alttestamentlicher Zeit*, Munich, 1973 (E.T., *A History of Israel in Old Testament Times*, 1975).
42. K.Koch, *Ratlos vor der Apokalyptik: Eine Streitschrift*, Gütersloh, 1970 (E.T., *The Rediscovery of Apocalyptic*, 1972).
43. Ibid., "Spätisraelitisches Geschichtsdenken am Beispiel des Buches Daniel," *Historische Zeitschrift*, 193-1, 1961, pp. 1-32.
44. H.J. Kraus, *Geschichte der historisch-kritischen Erforschung des Alten Testaments*, Neukirchen, ²1969.
45. J. Maier, J. Schreiner (Hg.), *Literatur und Religion des Frühjudentums: Eine Einführung*, Würzburg, 1973.
46. Ed. Meyer, *Geschichte des Altertums*, 2 Band, 2 Abt., "Der Orient vom zwölften bis zur Mitte des achten Jahrhunderts," Darmstadt, ³1953.
47. M. Metzger, *Grundriss der Geschichte Israels*, Neukirchen, 1976.
48. H. P. Müller, *Mythos, Tradition, Revolution, Phänomenologische Untersuchungen zum Alten Testament*, Neukirchen, 1973.
49. M. Noth, "Das Geschichtsverständnis der alttestamentlichen Apokalyptik," *Ges. Studien z. Alten Testament*, Munich, 1966 (E.T., *The Laws in the Pentateuch and Other Studies*, pp. 194-214).
50. Ibid., pp. 274-90 (E.T., pp. 215-28).

51. Ibid., *Geschichte Israels*, Göttingen, [6]1966 (E.T., *The History of Israel*, 1958).

52. O. Plöger, *Theokratie und Eschatologie*, Neukirchen, [3]1968 (E.T., *Theocracy and Eschatology*, 1968).

53. G. von Rad, *Theologie des Alten Testaments*, Bd. 1&2, Munich, [6]1969, 1975 (E.T., *Old Testament Theology*, New York, 1962-65, 2 vols.).

54. Ibid., "Der Anfang der Geschichtsschreibung im alten Israel," *Ges. Studien z. Alten Testament*, Munich, 1958, pp. 148-88 (E.T., *The Problem of the Hexateuch and Other Essays*, 1966, pp. 166-204).

55. D. Rössler, *Gesetz und Geschichte: Untersuchungen zur Theologie der jüdischen Apokalyptik und der pharisäischen Orthodoxie*, Neukirchen, 1960.

56. W. H. Schmidt, *Alttestamentlicher Glaube in seiner Geschichte*, Neukirchen, 1975.

57. R. Smend, *Elemente alttestamentlichen Geschichtsdenkens*, Theol. Studien Heft 95, Zürich, 1968.

58. K. Seybold, *Bilder zum Tempelbau: Die Visionen des Propheten Sacharja*, Stuttgarter Bibelstudien 70, 1974.

59. W. Zimmerli, *Grundriss der alttestamentlichen Theologie*, Stuttgart, 1972 (E.T., *Old Testament Theology in Outline*, 1978).

III. Philosophy of History

60. E. Bloch, *Das Prinzip Hoffnung*, Gesamtausgabe Bd. 5, Frankfurt/M., 1959.

61. Th. Bowman, *Das hebräische Denken im Vergleich mit dem Griechischen*, Göttingen, [2]1954, [4]1965 (E.T., *Hebrew Thought Compared with Greek*, 1960).

62. G. Delling, *Das Zeitverständnis des Neuen Testaments*, Gütersloh, 1940.

63. E. Dinkler (Hg.), *Zeit und Geschichte: Dankesgabe an Rudolf Bultmann*, Tübingen, 1964.

64. *Eranos-Jahrbuch*, 1951, Bd. 20: "Mensch und Zeit," Zürich, 1952.

65. J. Finegan, *Handbook of Biblical Chronology: Principles of Time Reckoning in the Ancient World and Problems of Christology in the Bible*, Princeton, 1964.

66. H. G. Gadamer, *Wahrheit und Methode: Grundzüge einer*

philosophischen Hermeneutik, Tübingen, 1965 (E.T., *Truth and Method*, 1975).

67. A.H. Gardiner, *The Admonitions of an Egyptian Sage*, Leipzig, 1909, rev. ed. Hildesheim, 1969 (Egyptian text with English translation and commentary).

68. F. Gogarten, "Das abendländische Geschichtsdenken: Bemerkungen zu dem Buch von Erich Auerbach 'Mimesis,' " *ZTK* 51, 1954, pp. 270-360.

69. K. Gründer, *Figur und Geschichte: Johann Georg Hamanns "Biblischen Betrachtungen" als Ansatz einer Geschichtsphilosophie*, Symposium 3, Freiburg/Munich, 1958.

70. W.Helck, *Die Prophezeiung des Nfr.*, Wiesbaden, 1970.

71. W.Helck, W. Westendorf, *Lexikon der Ägyptologie II*, Lfg. 4, Wiesbaden, 1976, pp. 559-68.

72. H.Köhler, *Geist und Geschichte*, Die Humboldt-Bücherei Bd. 10, Leipzig, 1948.

73. H.Lietzmann, *Zeitrechnung der römischen Kaiserzeit, des Mittelalters und der Neuzeit für die Jahre 1-2000 n. Chr.*, GöschenBd. 1085, Berlin, 1946, ³1956.

74. K.Löwith, *Weltgeschichte und Heilsgeschehen: Die theologischen Voraussetzungen der Geschichtsphilosophie*, Urban-Bücher 2, Stuttgart, ⁵1964 (E.T., *Meaning in History*, 1949).

75. J. Moltmann, *Theologie der Hoffnung*, Munich, 1964 (E.T., *Theology of Hope*, 1967).

76. S. Morenz, *Ägyptische Religion*, Stuttgart, 1960, pp. 65-84 (E.T., *Egyptian Religion*, 1973).

77. S. Morenz, D. Müller, *Untersuschungen zur Rolle des Schicksals in der ägyptischen Religion*, Abh. d. Sächs. Akad. d. Wiss., Leipzig, Phil. hist. Kl. 52, 1, Berlin, 1960.

78. M.P. Nilsson, *Geschichte der griechischen Religion*, 2 Bd., Munich, 1950 (E.T., *A History of Greek Religion*, 1949).

79. E. Otto, "Altägyptische Zeitvorstellungen und Zeitbegriffe," *Die Welt als Geschichte*, 14, 1954, pp. 135ff.

80. Ibid., "Zeitvorstellungen und Zeitrechnung im Alten Orient," *Studium Generale*, 19, 1966, pp. 743-51.

81. Ibid., *Der Verwurf an Gott: Zur Entstehung der ägyptischen Auseinandersetzungsliteratur*, Hildesheim, 1951.

81a. Ibid., *Wesen und Wandel der ägyptischen Kultur*, Verständlich Wissenschaft Bd., 100 Berlin, Heidelberg, 1969.

82. W.F. Otto, *Die Götter Griechenlands: Das Bild des Göttlichen*

im Spiegel des griechischen Geistes, Frankfurt/M., 1947 (E.T., *The Homeric Gods,* 1954).

83. C. H. Ratschow, "Anmerkungen zur theologischen Auffassung des Zeitproblems," *ZTK* 51, 1954, pp. 360-87.

84. J. B. Pritchard (Hg.), *Ancient Near-Eastern Texts Relating to the Old Testament,* Princeton, ³1969.

85. G. Sauter, *Zukunft und Verheissung: Das Problem der Zukunft in der gegenwärtigen theologischen und philosophischen Diskussion,* Zürich/Stuttgart, 1965.

86. F. Schiller, "Was heisst und zu welchem Ende studiert man Universalgeschichte? Eine akademische Antrittsrede," *Schillers Werke,* hg. von Witkop und Kühnemann, 10 Bd., Berlin, n.d., 207-26.

87. W. Zimmerli, *Der Mensch und seine Hoffnung im Alten Testaments,* Göttingen, 1968 (E.T., *Man and His Hope in the Old Testament,* 1971).

IV. Theology of History

88. Ed. Heimann, *Theologie der Geschichte: Ein Versuch,* Stuttgart Berlin, 1966.

89. F. Hesse, *Abschied von der Heilsgeschichte,* Theol. Studien, 108, Zürich, 1971.

90. H. Köhler, *Trinität und Geschichte: Eine Theologische Deutung der Geschichte,* Munich, 1969.

91. Ibid., *Christliche Existenz in säkularer und totalitärer Welt: Ein Beitrag aus der Sicht evangelischer Theologie,* Munich, 1963.

92. A. Dedo Müller, "Die Erkenntnisfunktion des Glaubens," *Schriften der Evang. Forschungsakademie,* Ilsenburg Heft 10, Berlin, 1952.

93. Ibid., *Dämonische Wirklichkeit und Trinität: Der Atomkrieg als theologisches Problem: Meditation und Strukturanalyse,* Gütersloh, 1963.

94. W. Pannenberg (Hg.), *Offenbarung als Geschichte,* Göttingen, ³1965 (E.T., *Revelation as History,* 1968).

95. R. Rendtorff, "Hermeneutik des Alten Testaments als Frage nach der Geschichte," *Ges. Studien zum Alten Testament,* Munich, 1975, pp. 11-24.

96. H. Thielicke, *Geschichte und Existenz: Grundlegung einer evangelischen Geschichtstheologie,* Gütersloh, 1964.

B. The Historical Images

I. Old Testament

97. H. Gese, "Geschichtliches Denken im Alten Orient und im Alten Testament," *Vom Sinai zum Zion*, Munich, 1974, pp. 81-98.
98. S. Herrmann, *Prophetie und Wirklichkeit in der Epoche des babylonischen Exils*, Berlin/Stuttgart, 1967.
99. M. Noth, *Uberlieferungsgeschichtliche Studien: Die sammelnden und bearbeitenden Geschichtswerke im Alten Testament*, Halle, 1943.
100. E. Otto, "Geschichtsbild und Geschichtsschreibung in Ägypten," *Die Welt des Orients*, Bd. III, 1964-66, 161-76.
101. G. von Rad, "Das formgeschichtliche Problem des Hexateuch," *Ges. Studien z. Alten Testament*, Munich, 1958, pp. 9-86 (E.T., *The Problem of the Hexateuch and Other Essays*, 1966, pp. 1-78).
102. R. Rendtorff, "Geschichte und Uberlieferung," *Ges. Studien z. Alten Testament*, Munich, 1975, pp. 25-38.
103. L. Rost, "Das kleine geschichtliche Credo," *Das kleine Credo und andere Studien zum Alten Testament*, Heidelberg, 1965.
104. B. Spuler (Hg.), *Handbuch der Orientalistik*, I. 1,2: "Ägyptologie/Literatur," Leiden/Köln, ²1970, pp. 139-47; E. Otto, "Welt-anschauliche und politische Tendenzschriften," pp. 169-79; E. Otto, "Annalistik und Königsnovelle," pp. 179-88; E. Otto, "Biographen."
105. W. Zimmerli, "Alttestamentliche Traditionsgeschichte und Theologie," *Ges. Aufsätze II*, Munich, 1974, pp. 9-26.

II. New Testament

106. O. Cullmann, *Christus und die Zeit: Die urchristliche Zeit und Geschichtsauffassung*, Zürich, 1946 (E.T., *Christ and Time*, 1950).
107. E. Fuchs, W. Künneth, *Die Auferstehung Jesus Christi von den Toten: Die Disputation von Sittensen*, Neukirchen, 1973.
108. H. Gese, "Natus ex virgine," *Vom Sinai zum Zion*, Munich, 1974, pp. 130-46.
109. E. Grässler, *Die Naherwartung Jesu*, Stuttgarter Bibelstudien, 61, 1973.

110. Ibid., "Motive und Methoden der neueren Jesus-Literatur: An Beispielen dargestellt," *Verkündigung und Forschung*, 18, 1973, pp. 3-44.

111. S. Herrmann, "Prophetie und Aktaulität: Biblische Denkstrukturen in ihrer Begegnung mit abendländischer Geistigkeit," *Theologie in Geschichte und Kunst*, Festschrift W. Elliger, Witten, 1968, pp. 61-73.

112. J. Jeremias, *Neutestamentliche Theologie*, I, Gütersloh, ²1973 (E.T., *New Testament Theology*, I, 1971).

113. Ibid., *Das Problem des historichen Jesus*, Calwer Hefte 32, Stuttgart, ⁵1966 (E.T., *The Problem of the Historical Jesus*, 1964).

114. W.G. Kümmel, *Verheissung und Erfüllung: Untersuchungen zur eschatologischen Verkündigung Jesu*, Zürich, ³1967 (E.T., *Promise and Fulfillment*, 1957).

115. Ibid., "Ein Jahrzehnt Jesusforschung (1965–1975)," *Theologische* Rundschau 40, 1975, pp. 289-336.

116. U. Luz, *Das Geschichtsverständnis des Paulus*, Munich, 1968.

117. W. Marxsen, *Die Sache Jesu geht weiter*, Gütersloher Taschenbücher 112, n.d.

118. Ibid., U. Wilckens, G. Delling, H.J. Geyer, *Die Bedeutung der Auferstehungsbotschaft für den Glauben an Jesus Christus*, Gütersloh, 1966.

119. Ibid., *Anfangsprobleme der Christologie*, Gütersloh, ²1964 (E.T., *The Beginnings of Christology*, 1969).

120. F. Mussner, *Die Auferstehung Jesu*, Munich, 1969.

121. R.R. Niebuhr, *Auferstehung und geschichtliches Denken*, Gütersloh, 1960 (E.T., *Resurrection and Historical Reason*, 1957).

122. K.H. Rengstorf, *Die Auferstehung Jesu: Form, Art und Sinn der urchristlichen Osterbotschaft*, Witten/Berlin, ⁵1967.

123. H. Ristow, K. Matthiae (Hg.), *Der historische Jesus und der kerygmatische Christus: Beiträge zum Christusverständnis in Forschung und Verkündigung*, Berlin, ³1964.

124. L. Rost, "Alttestamentliche Wurzeln der ersten Auferstehung," *Studien zum Alten Testament*, Stuttgart, 1974, pp. 61-65.

125. M. Simon, *Die jüdischen Sekten zur Zeit Christi*, Einsiedeln, 1964 (E.T., *Jewish Sects at the Time of Jesus*, 1967).

126. H. Staudinger, *Die historische Glaubwürdigkeit der Evangelien*, Gladbeck/W., Würzburg, ³1974.

127. Ibid., *Gott: Fehlanzeige.? Überlegungen eines Historikers zu Grenzfragen seiner Wissenschaft*, Trier, 1968.
128. G. Steindorff, "Schillers Quelle für das 'Verschleite Bild zu Sais,' " *Zeitschrift für ägyptische Sprache und Altertumskunde* 69, 1933, pp. 71-72.
129. G. Strude (Hg.), *Wer war Jesus von Nazareth? Die Erforschung einer historischen Gestalt*, Munich, 1972.

Conclusions

130. F. Gogarten, *Verhängnis und Hoffnung der Neuzeit: Die Säkelarisierung als theologische Problem*, Stuttgart, ²1958.
131. R.W. Meyer (Hg.), *Das Problem des Fortschritts–heute*, Darmstadt, 1969.
132. D. von Oppen, *Das personale Zeitalter: Formen und Grundlagen gesellschaftlichen Lebens im 20 Jahrhundert*, Stuttgart, ⁴1965.
133. W. Scheel, "Was wir aus der Geschichte lernen müssen: Die bedenklich Situation des Geschichtsunterrichts." Aus der Rede des Bundes präsidenten beim Historikertag. *Frankfurter Allgemeine Zeitung*, 23, Sept. 1976, Nr. 213, p. 6.
134. P. Tillich, *Auf der Grenze*, Stuttgart, 1962.
135. H. Trümpy (Hg.), *Kontinuität—Diskontinuität in den Geisteswissenschaften*, Darmstadt, 1973.